THE REFERENCE SHELF (Continued)

Volume 26

No.
5. The Censorship of Books. 2d printing. W. M. Daniels. $2.

Volume 25

No.
3. Representative American Speeches: 1952-1953. A. C. Baird. $1.75.

Volume 24

3. Representative American Speeches: 1951-1952. A. C. Baird. $1.75.

Volume 23

No.
2. Representative American Speeches: 1950-1951. A. C. Baird. $1.75.

Volume 22

No.
3. Representative American Speeches: 1949-1950. A. C. Baird. $1.75.

Volume 20

No.
5. Federal World Government. J. E. Johnsen. $1.50.

Volume 18

No.
3. Representative American Speeches: 1944-1945. A. C. Baird $1.25.

THE REFERENCE SHELF

Vol. 31   No. 4

CANADA

Edited by
GLADYS ENGEL LANG

THE H. W. WILSON COMPANY
NEW YORK   1959

19845

PREFACE

No other nation do Americans feel they "know" so well yet actually know so little about as their neighbor to the north, Canada. Americans, in general, show no great interest in Canadian affairs.

Lack of interest may result from a lack of tension in American-Canadian affairs. The two nations have been at peace since the War of 1812. Many Americans settle in Canada every year, and still more Canadians settle in the United States. Unfortunately it is trouble rather than its absence which hits the headlines and stimulates widespread interest in a foreign country.

A sense of familiarity also helps to account for this lack of interest. Americans assume that Canada is, though politically distinct, essentially similar to the United States in its way of life. For many, Canada is the one land of foreign travel, and there they find much that is familiar. In most of the country people speak English with a not unfamiliar accent, wear American clothes, like baseball, and watch American television programs.

Occasionally an American wonders aloud (sometimes in the American press) whether Canada might not do well to join the Union. This suggestion not only reveals an abysmal ignorance of Canada as an economic and political entity but offends the sensitivities of Canadians who are proud of their separate heritage. Geographically and economically Canadians are close to the United States. Sentimentally, and by reason of familial ties, many are closer to Britain or France. But their fundamental loyalty is to Canada.

Many Americans have lately been shaken into an awareness of Canadian affairs. The Liberal party, long in power, suffered a national defeat in which widespread anti-American sentiments appeared to play a decisive role. Selections in the first two sections of this compilation introduce the reader to the Canadian people and their government and the meaning of the recent shift in political power. How did it come about? What will be the effect on U.S.-Canadian relations? The third section reviews Canadian foreign policy, including Canada's relations with the United States and the Commonwealth. Some of the economic and social problems which challenge the Canadian people are discussed in Sections IV and V.

The compiler wishes to thank the various authors, publishers, and organizations that have granted permission for the use of materials included in this book.

GLADYS ENGEL LANG

June 1959

CONTENTS

PREFACE 3

Map: Canada 8

I. CANADA AND THE CANADIANS

Editor's Introduction 9

Canada's History 10

How Canada is Governed 14

Wrong, Dennis. Federal Power versus Provincial Autonomy 15

The Canadian People 18

Wrong, Dennis. The French Canadians 19

Filion, Gerard and Hatcher, Harlan. Americans and Canadians: A Comparison 25

II. THE CONSERVATIVES COME TO POWER

Editor's Introduction 30

Mutchmor, J. R. Canada's Parties ...... Christian Century 30

The Conservative Landslide .... Atlantic Monthly 32

Ferns, H. S. A New Course in Canadian Politics? ....
.... Political Quarterly 37

Bryden, Ken. A Party of Outsiders 44

III. CANADA, THE COMMONWEALTH AND THE WORLD

Editor's Introduction 47

Pearson, Lester B. The Crown and the Commonwealth ... 48

McKenty, Neil. A Brief Résumé of Foreign Policy ......
.... America 52

What Is a Middle Power? 55

Spencer, Robert A. Continuity in Foreign Policy 60

6   CONTENTS

Daniell, Raymond. Frontier of Understanding ....
.... New York Times   71

Brady, Alexander. Cooperation is Imperative   73

Kehoe, S. G. The DEW Line: Radar Frontier .. America   76

Jones, Gardiner B. Americans in Canada: Flying the DEW
Line .... New York Times Magazine   80

Nason, John. Areas of Tension: American Viewpoint   83

Glazebrook, George P. de T. Areas of Tension: Canadian
Viewpoint   87

Diefenbaker, John. Talk About Economic Relations .....
.... U. S. News & World Report   89

Swayze, Walter E. Against Anti-Americanism ....
.... Queen's Quarterly   97

IV. ECONOMIC GROWING PAINS

Editor's Introduction 105

Growing Pains of a Young Giant .... Economist 106

Boom Across the Border (1957) .... Senior Scholastic 108

Hills, Theo L. Natural Resources and Economic Potential 110

Friedlander, P. J. C. The St. Lawrence Seaway: What It Is
and What It Means .... New York Times 116

The Meaning For Canadian Ports .... Newsweek 121

Davey, Clark. The Meaning for Labrador's Ore ....
.... New York Times 125

Sullivan, Walter. The Arctic Potential ....
.... New York Times Magazine 128

Canada's Social Needs .... Economist 135

Neuberger, Richard L. Family Allowances ...... America 138

V. DIVERSITY AND UNITY

Editor's Introduction 141

Eckerson, Helen F. Magnet for Immigration ... Annals of
the American Academy of Political and Social Sciences 142

CONTENTS

Barkway, Michael. Turning Point for Immigration? 146

Immigrants and the North .... Economist 150

Belliveau, J. E. Newcomers and the Cities ...... America 153

Wrong, Dennis. Social Discrimination 156

Schools: Public But Separate .. U.S. News & World Report 159

The Plastic Igloo .... Economist 161

Butz, Otto. Can Canadian Culture Survive? ....
.... Antioch Review 164

MacLuhan, Marshall. Defrosting Canadian Culture ......
.... American Mercury 169

Unity Via Video .... Citizenship Items 173

Long, Tania. Promoting Canadian Talent ....
.... New York Times 176

BIBLIOGRAPHY 179

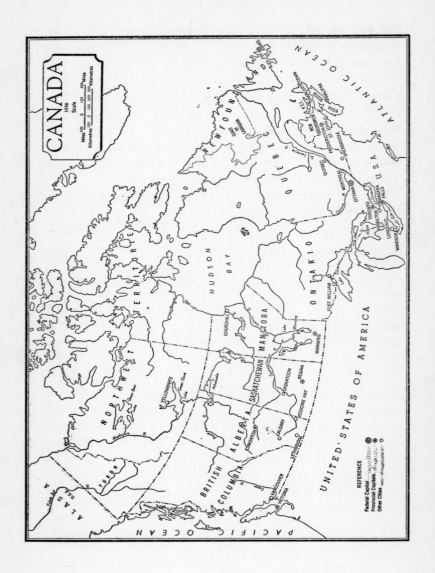

I. CANADA AND THE CANADIANS

EDITOR'S INTRODUCTION

Canada was first a colony of France, then of Great Britain. It has come into independent nationhood gradually and slowly and quite recently. Only in 1949 did the Canadian Parliament officially gain the right to amend its own constitution.

This evolution into nationhood is reviewed in the first article of this section. The remaining selections supply some background on the government and people of Canada. The heritage of the past has plainly left its mark. Canada, as the second article points out, retains a formal tie to the British crown. Its Parliament is modeled closely on the British parliamentary system. Yet as sociologist Dennis Wrong points out in the third article, the Canadian party system, in spite of its formal resemblance to the British system, is in many respects more like that of the United States. Moreover, the American distinction between states' rights and federal power is roughly similar to the Canadian split between federal power and provincial autonomy.

As the fourth selection shows, Canada's people come from many lands but Canada's dual inheritance is reflected in its two major language groups: the French-speaking and English-speaking Canadians. Professor Wrong, in the article which follows, argues that there has been national union but not national unity; the traditional loyalty of the French-speaking Canadian has been to his own people rather than to the Canadian Confederation. In the exchange between an American and a French Canadian recorded in the final selection it is noted that there may be greater diversity within Canada than between Canada and the United States.

CANADA'S HISTORY [1]

The origins of Canada are to be found in the period, three and a half centuries ago, when the European states were establishing colonies outside the old world. There were four points of entry to the interior of North America, and England and France each chose two. The English made settlements midway on the Atlantic coast in Virginia and New England; and penetrated the difficult waters of Hudson Bay to the southern tip. The French voyaged to what is now Nova Scotia and up the St. Lawrence River; later they sailed through the Gulf of Mexico to the mouth of the Mississippi River and founded New Orleans. Thus the early history of Canada for over a century was as a French colony.

Two main themes may be seen in the history of New France: the creation of agricultural communities in Acadia (Nova Scotia) and the St. Lawrence Valley, and, partly complementary and partly competing, expansion to the west of the continent with the objectives of enlarging the trade in furs, of converting the Indians to Christianity, and of carving out a great empire as an adjunct in the New World to the ambitions of the Bourbon kings in Europe. The first precarious settlements were made by Samuel de Champlain at Port Royal in Acadia and at Quebec on the St. Lawrence River. As was the fashion of the day, the responsibility was first placed in companies chartered by the Crown, companies which drew their revenues from the fur trade and in return were obligated to bring settlers. Since, however, the companies were more attracted by the former than the latter, New France was reorganized as a royal colony in 1663. Inevitably it reflected the character of metropolitan France. The form of government was autocratic, only the Roman Catholic religion was tolerated, and land was granted by feudal tenure. The conditions of frontier life, however, forced governors to make important modifications in the system with the result that neither the operation of government nor the attenuated feudalism in

[1] From *Fact Sheet*, no. 4, information bulletin. Canada. Department of External Affairs. Information Division. Ottawa, Ontario. June 1957. Reprinted by permission.

New France created the discontent and grievances that were later to bring revolution in France itself.

The colonists organized the drive into the interior from the bases on the St. Lawrence River and particularly from Montreal, founded in 1642 at the junction of the St. Lawrence and Ottawa rivers. The various, and often mixed, motives for this expansion have already been indicated. The broad plan was to enclose the English colonies by a great arc running through the Great Lakes and down the Mississippi; to find a way to the "western sea" and so to China; and to destroy the posts of the Hudson's Bay Company to the North. It was an ambitious and dramatic policy which had a degree of success remarkable in view of the small population that attempted it, and of the terrain itself.

By its very purpose, however, the French design assumed a continuing conflict with the English colonies. This conflict was made even more bitter when the Anglo-French rivalry in Europe was added. The Seven Years' War brought the end of French rule in Canada, Acadia having been already lost in 1713. For a few years the established colonies of Newfoundland, Nova Scotia (including the modern New Brunswick and Prince Edward Island) and Quebec—the original elements of modern Canada—were but the poorer portion of the great British Empire in North America. The successful American Revolution, however, created an independent country in the southern half of the continent, and left in question the future of the northern half.

The answers to that multiple question could by no means be assumed at the time, but may for a moment be anticipated here. The territory to the north of the United States was explored and possessed from the Atlantic colonies, the colony on the St. Lawrence, and through Hudson Bay. Unlike the other European colonies in the Americas, Canada did not revolt from its two European mother countries. It was severed politically from France in the eighteenth century; with the United Kingdom, it worked out a developing and mutually satisfactory relationship. Nor were the colonies that became Canada absorbed by the United States, although until the third quarter of the nineteenth century there was reason to fear forcible annexation, and even later there were those, on both sides of the boundary, who argued that Canada could not, in its own interest, remain a separate country.

For more than half a century after the American Revolution the colonies that together formed British North America were politically separated from each other. During that time their problems were many. Except in the earlier-settled parts of Quebec and Nova Scotia, the colonies were engaged in pioneer settlements made up largely of political émigrés from the United States who came to Canada as a result of the American Revolution. Later immigrants came from the British Isles and Europe as well as from the United States. To the fisheries, fur trade, and agriculture, were added lumbering, ship-building, and some manufacturing. Roads were cut, and railways began. War with the United States in 1812 interfered with these peaceful developments, and, internally, a series of political disputes on the degree of authority to be exercised by the elected assemblies led to armed uprisings in two of the provinces in 1837.

By the middle of the century a number of factors encouraged a movement for political union of the various colonies. One of these was the feeling that the western territories should be joined to the eastern provinces. Successors to the French explorers had, by the end of the eighteenth century, made their way to the Arctic and Pacific oceans. A few years later a settlement was made on the Red River (at what was later the city of Winnipeg) and towns were begun on the Pacific Coast. A second factor was the desire to cooperate in the building of a railway from the Atlantic Coast to the central provinces. A third was the belief that political union would facilitate economic growth. Fourthly—an equally compelling reason—was the need for joint defense against attacks that then seemed possible from United States territory.

The British North America Act of 1867 created a new Canada, embracing four provinces: Quebec, Ontario, Nova Scotia and New Brunswick. It provided for a federal union and for the parliamentary system already practiced in the provinces, that is, cabinet—or in the Canadian phrase—responsible government. It also provided that further provinces could be added. By stages the coast-to-coast membership was completed by the additions of Manitoba (1870), British Columbia (1871), Prince Edward Island (1873), and Newfoundland (1949). Alberta and Saskatchewan moved from territorial to provincial status in 1905.

The huge area from Atlantic to Pacific, and from the American border to the Arctic was, at the beginning of the twentieth century, occupied by not much more than five million people. Already railways across the width of the country had been constructed, and were an important element in making possible the settlement of immigrants. Wheat became an important article of export, moving by railway and inland waters to seaboard. The war of 1914, in addition to calling forth a large contribution of men, food, and munitions, hastened economic development, and, in particular, diversification of the economy. It brought, too, a new stage in the British Empire, or as it was now coming to be called—the Commonwealth of Nations. Canada joined the League of Nations in her own right. In 1926 the report of the Imperial Conference described the equality of status of the self-governing members and the Statute of Westminster of 1931 gave legal form to that position.

Canada, then, entered the Second World War on her own initiative, and took an active part in it, and subsequently in the United Nations and the North Atlantic Treaty Organization. Diplomatic representation was rapidly increased to meet the requirements of the war and the events which followed it. Again, too, came another period of economic expansion following the world-wide depression of the thirties. Diversification was an important aspect, but the most striking one was the development of the northern areas made possible by the discoveries of minerals and by air transport. What had once been a fringe of population along the southern border began to spread . . . [north and west] toward the Arctic Ocean, a process which suggests new possibilities for the future.

HOW CANADA IS GOVERNED [2]

Canada has a democratic parliamentary system of government. Although, in the British North America Act, it possesses a form of written constitution, many of its legal and parliamentary practices stem from old unwritten British custom. The ten provinces of Canada are united under a federal government, which controls matters concerning the country as a whole —such as defense, trade and commerce, banking, transportation and external relations. The provincial governments have authority over such matters as education, property laws and health. Within the provinces, elected municipal bodies deal with local affairs.

Queen Elizabeth II, who stands as a symbol of free association among the nations of the Commonwealth, is, as Queen of Canada, the head of the Canadian State. Her representative in Canada is the Governor General, who is appointed on the recommendation of the Prime Minister, usually for a five-year term.

Parliament consists of the Queen, the Senate and the House of Commons. The Senate has 102 members, appointed on a regional basis by the Governor General on the advice of the Prime Minister, and holding office for life. The 265 members of the House of Commons are elected by the people of Canada for a nominal term of five years. The Prime Minister may, however, at any time advise the Governor General to dissolve Parliament and call a new election. If the Government loses the support of the majority in the House of Commons, it is obliged either to resign or to call another election.

After an election, the party with a majority in the House of Commons forms the Government. If, however, no party commands a majority, a government can be formed by the coalition of two or more parties, though this has seldom happened in Canada. The leader of the party that has most elected members normally becomes Prime Minister and chooses a Cabinet

[2] From *Fact Sheet*, no. 5, information bulletin. Canada. Department of External Affairs. Information Division. Ottawa, Ontario. June 1957.

from among his supporters in the House. He and his Cabinet colleagues are collectively responsible to the House of Commons. Cabinet ministers head the various government departments, which are staffed by civil servants retaining their positions no matter what party is in power. . . .

Although the Senate possesses the power to reject any but a money bill, it rarely does so. Before a bill can become law, it must be signed by the Governor General. It would, however, be contrary to long established constitutional practice (based on the unwritten custom already mentioned) for the Governor General to withhold his signature from any measure adopted by the two chambers of Parliament.

Except in Quebec, which has an appointed Legislative Council as well as an elected Legislative Assembly, the provincial legislatures consist of single chambers. . . . In each province, a lieutenant-governor is appointed by the federal government as the representative of the Crown.

The Yukon and Northwest Territories are governed by commissioners appointed by the federal government, assisted by territorial councils.

FEDERAL POWER VERSUS PROVINCIAL AUTONOMY [3]

The difference between the Canadian parliamentary system, modeled on the British, and the American tripartite division of governmental powers established by the Constitution is perhaps the most striking contrast that exists between the formal institutions of the two nations. Yet both Canadians and Americans define their countries first of all as democracies and equally cherish the principle of majority rule as the most desirable form of political organization. Canadians do not carry it quite as far as Americans and are often critical of the number of elective offices in the United States. Political democracy is seen as an orderly and traditionally workable system of government rooted

[3] From *American and Canadian Viewpoints*, pamphlet by Dennis Wrong, Canadian sociologist now at Brown University. American Council on Education. Washington, D.C. 1955. p33-66. Reprinted by permission.

in law and precedent rather than solely as an instrument for giving expression to the will of the people. American veneration of the Constitution is paralleled by Canadian reverence for parliamentary tradition and custom.

Canadians, like Americans, frequently display considerable disdain for professional politicians; yet at the same time they are readier to discount partisan passions and are more inclined to elevate their political leaders to the status of statesmen within the latter's lifetime, seeing them in the image of great British parliamentarians who lead rather than merely follow the nation. Suspicion of the "never-ending audacity of elected persons" is less acute in Canada than in the United States. Since the depression, however, the Canadian voter has increasingly tended in provincial elections to support parties other than those he votes for federally, although in the last federal election the western provinces voted federally for the first time in much the same way as they had voted in previous provincial elections. At present [1955] only four of the ten Canadian provinces have governments formed by the Liberal party that has been in power nationally since 1935. This pattern of voting suggests a desire, especially in Ontario and Quebec, to check the power of the federal government by balancing it with opposing provincial administrations jealous of their autonomy, and it clearly resembles the American pattern of voting differently in presidential and congressional elections. In three provinces relatively new political parties are in power. [See Section II.]

In spite of its formal resemblance to the British system, the Canadian party system is in many respects more like that of the American. The two major parties do not present the voter with a clear-cut choice between a rightist and a leftist program; like the Republican and Democratic parties, their support comes from diverse economic, regional, and ethnic voting blocs whose often conflicting aims and interests must be skillfully compromised. The campaign tactics of Canadian politicians, therefore, usually resemble those of their American counterparts. Political oratory is somewhat more subdued in tone in Canada and national elections do not hold the center of the stage as completely or inspire as intense emotions. This results largely from the existence of more deeply rooted sectional loyalties in Canada where the provinces tend to be larger than American states and coincide more closely with geographic regions. Shifts in public attitude that are nation-wide in scope are not as common in Canada as in the United States where, as indicated by voting behavior, the nation increasingly tends to respond as a whole to public affairs. The Canadian conflict between the defenders of provincial autonomy and the advocates of greater federal powers resembles the controversies over states' rights in the United States. Both struggles have their origins in federal political systems differing widely in detail but which are in broad outline very similar products of the North American environment.

"Democracy" to French-speaking Canadians is understood primarily as a political concept referring to a system of government that has preserved their minority rights and interests within the Canadian confederation. They have been, therefore, possibly the most active defenders of the articles of confederation, of provincial as against federal autonomy, and of the autonomy of the federal Parliament as against the British government. . . .

French-Canadian nationalist aspirations have played a considerable part in Canadian politics. In their most extreme form, held only by a small though influential minority, they have envisaged the creation of an independent French-speaking nation to be called "Laurentia" on the shores of the St. Lawrence. However, with the closer economic integration of Quebec and the rest of Canada this dream has lost much of its influence. More commonly, French-Canadian nationalism is expressed in determined resolutions to preserve the French language and the traditional culture of Catholic Quebec from the inroads of English-speaking Canadian commercialism (often called "imperialism" in Quebec) and from the influence of American habits and attitudes communicated by the mass media from across the border. Politically, French-Canadian nationalism has insisted on the maintenance of provincial autonomy and has resisted involvement in overseas wars, although the intense hostility to communism in French-speaking Canada has reduced her traditional isolationism in the present world crisis.

THE CANADIAN PEOPLE [4]

What kind of people are Canadians?

Like the residents of the United States, Canadians are energetic, ambitious and productive. When it comes to shop talk, the two peoples understand each other very well. Production records, for example, are something to be made today and broken tomorrow. Canadians and Americans both draw inspiration from the drama of business and industry, and the pioneer instinct still is strong on both sides of the border.

Canada's population of more than 15 million can be roughly divided into three main groups—English and French, and a third composite group of other European peoples and Americans. Both English and French are official languages in Canada. Persons of British stock account for slightly less than one-half Canada's population. Included in this group are the descendants of immigrants from the British Isles; of the United Empire Loyalists who migrated to Canada after the American Revolution, and more recent settlers from the United States and the United Kingdom.

Over 30 per cent of Canadians are of French stock. Most of them are descended from French colonists who remained in Canada when it came under British rule in 1763. While more than a million French Canadians are scattered throughout Canada, most live in the Province of Quebec. Here they have retained a distinctive way of life which is guaranteed and respected by the Canadian government.

The third segment of the Canadian population arrived with the wave of settlement which swept over the West during the first two decades of this century. Immigration declined between World War I and II, but has increased sharply since 1945. Today, nearly one-fifth of Canada's population is made up of persons of Ukrainian, Scandinavian, German, Dutch, and Polish

[4] From *Our Partnership With Canada,* Information Bulletin distributed by the United States Chamber of Commerce as background on issues in the news. (Bulletin no 34) United States Chamber of Commerce. Washington 6, D.C. July 20, 1954. p4-5. Reprinted by permission.

origin. They are concentrated mainly in the prairie provinces—Manitoba, Saskatchewan and Alberta.

In religion, too, Canada is diverse. About 40 per cent of the population are Roman Catholic, and about two-thirds of this group are French Canadians. Second largest religious group is the United Church of Canada, formed in 1925 by the union of Canadian Methodists, Congregationalists and some Presbyterians. The Church of England in Canada constitutes the third religious group. Numerous other faiths including Hebrew, Greek Orthodox and Mormon are found across the country.

How big is Canada?

Canada includes the whole northern half of the North American continent except Alaska—a total area of 3,845,774 square miles. Canada is slightly larger than continental United States and Alaska combined, and only somewhat smaller than the whole of Europe, including European Russia. . . .

In population, Canada has made a five-fold expansion since she officially came into being eighty-six years ago, and there are predictions that she will triple her present population . . . within the next half century. Immigration accounts for part of these increases, while Newfoundland's entry into the Confederation of 1949 added another 350,000 persons. The major source of increases, however, has been natural expansion. During the century 1851-1951, births exceeded deaths by 11 million.

By far the majority of Canadians live in the border area between Canada and the United States, although in recent years there has been some expansion northward.

THE FRENCH CANADIANS [5]

Roughly one-third of the Canadian population is French-speaking.

French-speaking Canadians are not, as many Americans believe, a "minority group" faced with the prospect of being

[5] From *American and Canadian Viewpoints*, pamphlet by Dennis Wrong, Canadian sociologist now at Brown University. American Council on Education, Washington, D.C. 1955. p3, p 11-13, p 15-16. Reprinted by permission.

"assimilated" by the majority like immigrant groups of European origin, but are equal partners with English-speaking Canadians in the Canadian confederation. The Canadian Constitution provides French-speaking Canadians with guarantees that their language shall share official status with English and gives them the right to maintain a state-supported Roman Catholic school system. These rights were first guaranteed to the French in Canada by the Quebec Act of 1774 following the British conquest, and thus antedate the formation of the Canadian nation in 1867 by nearly a century. In conjunction with French-speaking Canadian determination to preserve their cultural distinctiveness, they present formidable barriers to assimilation, which, indeed, has not been a real possibility at any time in Canadian history. . . .

To the French Canadian the family is not simply the sphere of "private life," but is considered to be the basic social unit and, accordingly, a major concern of society rather than an area to be left to the direction of individual choice and impulse. Stable family relations are regarded as the foundation of the entire religious, moral, and political order. The precepts governing family life are based on religious commandments and their fulfillment is equated with conformity to Divine intent. In accordance with the teachings of the Catholic Church, both divorce and birth control are condemned and motherhood is regarded as woman's crowning achievement. It is the duty of the individual to marry and procreate, provided he has the means to support a large family. In recent years the Church has adopted a more liberal attitude toward the sexual problems of marriage and in a number of Catholic higher educational institutions it now sponsors courses designed to prepare young people for marriage that include thorough instruction in sexual matters.

Kinship obligations loom large in the life of the French Canadians. Blood relations and in-laws are not remote figures as in many American and English-speaking Canadian families, but are a concrete group with which the individual remains identified throughout his lifetime. Brothers and sisters who have left home are asked on occasion to come back to help out in the house, on the farm, or running the family business. In rural Quebec the household group itself often includes members of several generations and marriage sometimes seems to be as much a union between two lineal families as between an individual man and woman. In contrast to the American pattern, occupations tend to be passed down from one generation to the next; a doctor or lawyer is expected to educate at least one of his sons to follow in his footsteps. The individualism with which French Canadians are often credited is really an individualism of families rather than of single persons, for the kinship group tends to be the center of the French Canadian's universe and he is often highly suspicious of all outsiders and prefers to be dependent only on "his own."

By tradition women are expected to remain in the home, but this is changing as more and more married and single women have found employment in the new factories and offices that have sprung up in the last twenty years. In the past the husband was regarded as the supreme authority over both wife and children; some French Canadians even attacked the Federal Family Allowances Act passed during World War II solely on the grounds that payments were to be made to mothers rather than to fathers. [See "Family Allowances" in Section IV, below.—Ed.] The father attempts to plan the careers of his children when they are still at an early age, and the obligation of supporting and educating them is his first financial responsibility. Only one son— not necessarily or even usually the eldest—inherits the farm or business, and the others have to be established on farms or as heads of businesses purchased for them, trained for the priesthood or another profession, or, in rural areas, sent to the city to seek less skilled employment, while the girls must find husbands or be educated to become nuns.

This pattern, which in most respects is essentially that of eighteenth-century France, has, however, been greatly modified by the urbanization and industrialization of the province and is becoming increasingly a thing of the past. While families are still large, the French-Canadian birth rate has fallen in response to the economic difficulties of supporting and finding occupations for a large number of children. The lack of new land to absorb the surplus rural population and the acute urban unemployment of the 1930's have challenged the basis of the system. The closeness of kinship ties and the subordinate position of women and children in the home are likely to diminish even more rapidly in the future, but the family, sanctified by religion, will undoubtedly remain the bedrock of French-Canadian existence. . . .

In French-speaking Canada religion is more than simply an attitude toward the universe or a set of conventional observances divorced from the rest of living; the Catholic Church is the dominant institutional authority, guiding and supervising the entire round of life. The Church sponsors organizations active in a large number of different fields, among them fraternal societies, youth organizations, savings and loan societies, charitable organizations, trade unions, and scouts. Traditionally, the family and the Catholic parish have been the most important and virtually the only organized social groups in the world of the rural French Canadian. But in the cities the parish has lost some of its former significance and Catholic associations organized on the basis of sex, age, and marital status, or to appeal to other groups with special interests, have assumed a more important role in relating the individual to the Church.

The French Canadians regard themselves as preservers of the traditional Catholicism that lost influence in the original mother country after the French Revolution. Catholicism is factually, if not formally, the established religion of the province of Quebec, and priests are the counselors of the community in much of the secular life as well as in religious matters. While priests often differ widely in their views on political and social questions—particularly with respect to relations between French-speaking and English-speaking Canada—organized Catholicism in Quebec has never been divided into Right, Left, and Center wings as in France and there has been little outright anticlericalism of the sort common in France which is often indistinguishable from anti-Catholicism. In the past decade, however, some French-Canadian intellectuals have become increasingly vocal in their opposition to the Church's supervision of extra-religious fields.

It is difficult to separate from one another the French Canadian's solicitude for his traditional faith and his pride in his people, most often expressed by his resolution to maintain the French language on a continent of English-speaking neighbors.

As Mason Wade has pointed out [in his book *The French Canadians, 1760-1945*], the French Canadian often disguises his nationalism as a vigorous concern for the preservation of his Catholicism; French Canadians have even maintained that the retention of their faith requires the continued use of the French language, a remarkable claim in view of the international and multilingual character of the Roman Catholic Church. Some observers have noted that French-Canadian audiences often applaud references to their "race" and their tongue far more enthusiastically than they do references to their Catholicism. The antagonism of much of the clergy to English-speaking Catholics, particularly the Irish, also suggests a blending of religious and national sentiment in which the latter often appears to be the more profoundly felt. Racist theories that construct a sharp polarity between the "Latin" attributes of the French Canadian and the "Anglo-Saxon" attributes of "the others" are widely held by members of the elite in Quebec and further contravene the prevalent English-speaking Canadian view that Catholicism alone is responsible for French-Canadian ethnic solidarity. In Wade's words ". . . racism is just as much confused with religion in Quebec as religion is with racism in English Canada." Religion is but one web—albeit probably the most important one next to language—of the network of ideals, attitudes, and customs that the French Canadian values as his "way of life" and wishes to protect against outside influences. Yet it has been so inextricably bound up with all of the components of the French-Canadian outlook that it is indeed difficult to tell where Catholicism ends and ethnic pride begins. As the urbanization and industrialization of Quebec continue, however, the ethnic sentiments and interests will probably become more distinguishable from the Catholic. . . .

The French-speaking Canadian outlook on international affairs bears a superficial resemblance to American isolationism, although its historical roots are quite different. The traditional loyalty of the French-speaking Canadian has been to his own people rather than to the Canadian confederation, or to North America as a whole. Wishing to preserve his language and his culture on a continent of English-speaking "strangers," he has been an isolationist with respect to the rest of Canada and to the United States, as well as in his attitude toward Europe.

Memories of the British conquest and fears of the cultural imperialism of English-speaking Canada have fostered a pronounced antipathy for involvement in "Britain's wars"—a phrase that carries echoes of the days when Canada had no independent foreign policy. The greatest strains in French-English relations have resulted from French-Canadian opposition to universal military conscription for overseas duty in both world wars, and "the national union which can probably never become a national unity" has looked its most unworkable on these occasions.

Indifferent if not antagonistic toward the imperial ties, respectful of the monarchic tradition without feeling close identification with the British Crown and royal family, critical of too close a tie with France—suspect on account of her anticlericalism—and fearful of American influences disrupting their way of life, French-speaking Canadians have mainly desired to be left alone to live their own lives in their beloved homeland of Quebec. French-speaking Canadian isolationism springs from this desire. Unlike American isolationism, it has not involved a wider concept of "Fortress America," or of the hemispheric solidarity expressed in the Monroe Doctrine, although during the 1930's the speeches of leading American isolationists like Senator Taft were widely quoted in the French-language press to justify non-involvement in the mounting European crisis.

In recent years the change in French-Canadian attitudes toward the outside world has been not unlike that which has taken place among former isolationist elements in the United States. There is a growing though reluctant recognition of Canada's unavoidable participation in world affairs. The Church's profound antagonism to communism has made the transition somewhat easier now that Russia has become the main opponent of the Anglo-Saxon nations and of France. Before World War II, on the other hand, a good many French Canadians sympathized with Franco's rebels in the Spanish Civil War, Mussolini's corporate state had some clerical supporters, and after the fall of France the Pétain regime also appealed to some French Canadians with its slogan of "Famille, Patrie, Travail" that replaced the despised "Liberté, Egalité, Fraternité" of the Republic and revolutionary France.

Growing national consciousness throughout Canada and the final severance of some remaining political and symbolic ties with Great Britain have reduced the French Canadian's distaste for involvement in what he has in the past called "Britain's wars." Indeed, French-Canadian attitudes, by exerting a powerful influence on national policy, have played a large part in reducing the influence of Downing Street on Ottawa and in encouraging Canada to assume complete control of her external relations. Probably, however, French-Canadian opposition to compulsory conscription would still be strong in the event of a third world war with Russia, for the issue has acquired a symbolic significance, arousing the group consciousness of the French-speaking Canadians to resist domination by Ottawa and by public opinion in English-speaking Canada.

AMERICANS AND CANADIANS: A COMPARISON [6]

[Gerard Filion:] We don't have the same concept of the family on both sides of the border, nor do we in English and French Canada.

In the United States, the family is a private affair between a man and a woman and eventually children. Divorce is generally accepted by most people, except Roman Catholics. Equality of husband and wife is enforced by law, though a large proportion of wives actually accept some kind of male authority. Nevertheless, family life is highly valued and flourishing in large sections of the American population.

The same appreciation of family life is widespread in English-speaking Canada.

French Canadians have retained a pattern of family life close to the concept commonly accepted in Europe. They take the

[6] From "The Canadian-American Community of Interest in Social and Educational Affairs," remarks by Gerard Filion, editor of *Le Devoir* in Montreal, and by Harlan Hatcher, president of the University of Michigan. In *Report of the Canada-United States Conference on Mutual Relations, Washington, D.C., February 7-8, 1955.* American Council on Education. Washington, D.C. 1955. p35-9; 40-5. Reprinted by permission.

family as the basic cell of the whole society and they make every effort to protect it from outside influences. The father retains a strong authority over every member of the group, since he is responsible for the material and intellectual welfare of the family. Even in the large industrial centers, the family in French Canada has retained many traditions and behaviors pertaining to the old patriarchal way of life. It should be said however that rapid changes are being experienced in family life in French Canada, but it cannot be expected that everywhere in North America people will ever face marriage and family life from the same point of view. . . .

No caste system is accepted by law or by tradition in North America. It must be pointed out, however, that both French-speaking and English-speaking Canada admit some kind of hierarchy in society. Emphasis is often put on the role played by the elite, this term being accepted in the wide sense of persons or groups of persons whose education, skill, intellectual value, and even birth indicate them as natural leaders of their fellow citizens. In French Canada more emphasis is put on authority than on liberty, and this attitude is often interpreted as a natural taste for fascist methods of government.

In the United States, equality of all citizens, not only in connection with law and personal rights, but with opportunities in professions and business, is deeply rooted in the mentality of the country. Democracy is not only a way of government but a way of life. The American believes in the common man and is proud to prove this with instances showing that a plain ordinary man may become president of the republic. . . .

In Anglo-Saxon countries, emphasis is strongly put on public schools as an indisputed right of the State to educate good citizens according to majority standards.

In Roman Catholic countries, it is generally assumed that parents have a natural and practically exclusive right to choose the kind of education to be given to their children, the Church and the State having only a substitute right when parents do not or cannot afford to perform their duty.

In the United States and English-speaking Canada, the education is mostly vocational, the nonutilitarian learning losing ground even in universities which are supposed to have the function of teaching knowledge for its own sake.

In French Canada, emphasis is put on culture as a means to achieve a superior type of men; this culture is based on a long and strenuous study of Latin, Greek, and philosophy, with a few hours left to techniques and sciences. It should be said however that a need for a more practical education is being felt among French Canadians during recent years. Technical schools and engineering departments of universities have been extensively improved since the last war.

Daily papers, magazines, pictures, radio and TV programs from south of the forty-fifth parallel are extensively read, seen, and heard in Canada. In English-speaking Canada, people are strongly influenced by the American culture and American way of life. On both sides of the border, the same songs are sung, the same magazines are read, the same pictures and TV shows are looked at. For an outsider, it is not always easy to see the difference between an automobile worker of Detroit and of Windsor, a farmer of Manitoba and of North Dakota, a businessman of Toronto and of New York. Mass communications weigh heavily on Canadian culture and are a handicap to Canada's developing a genuine way of life. This concern was one of the main points of the Massey report. [*Report of the Royal Commission on National Development in the Arts, Letters, and Sciences.* Ottawa: Queen's Printer, 1951.]

Though protected by its own language and traditions, French Canada is strongly influenced by American culture.

[Harlan Hatcher:] Of course, you have observed . . . the emphasis . . . placed upon the differences that do exist between the United States and Canada. I have no disposition to try to minimize those differences for I have observed them myself. I remember an experience I had while living in the City of Quebec. . . . I called upon . . . a man deeply learned in the lore of Canada, particularly of Quebec. He suggested that I call his opposite number who represented the French Canadians. . . .

I called this distinguished representative of the French people on the telephone. He answered in French. I might possibly at that time have responded in kind, but I did not. I went to see

him and expressed interest in the greeting which he had given
to me over the telephone.

He said, "We French Canadians always answer the telephone
in French. If our caller speaks in English, we switch to English."

I made a remark about the quality of his English pronunci-
ation. He said, "It is a matter of distinct pride for us French
Canadians that although we can speak English flawlessly, we do
not do so. We give it enough of a French flavor so you will
know we are French Canadians." . . .

We ought to remember . . . that differences exist within
Canada itself that are far more marked than the differences that
exist between Canada and the United States. There are more
differences between the Canadians, let us say, of the Quebec area
and the Canadians in Manitoba and Saskatchewan, to my knowledge, than there are between any part of Canada and Washington or New York or Detroit. You will find no differences as
marked in the United States as those in Canada. If you go from
our north to southwest U.S.A., there are differences of course,
but not as sharp as those I have mentioned.

I am telling you this because, in order to understand the
question of mutual relationships, we have first to understand that
differences are differences not solely because one country is
Canada and the other is the United States. On the contrary,
we are far more apt to find differences that are sectional rather
than national. The latter are disappearing too, I might hasten to
add. . . . I have had pointed out to me time and again, particularly by the Canadians in the Ontario or Port Arthur-Fort Wayne
section, or out in the Far West, that the Canadians who are now
moving into the north and south of that country are much more
closely connected with the United States on the south than with
the Canada of the east.

On the American side, our awareness of Canada is somewhat
fragmentary. . . . A great many of our ancestors did leave New
England and the Eastern seaboard at the time of the American
Revolution because of their loyalty to the Crown, and went over
to live in Canada. Today, a very strong group of their descendants lives in Canada, particularly in Ontario. They are certainly

as strong in their historical ties to their area as are our own first families of Virginia. They have a society that meets regularly to make sure that the loyalist spirit is not lost in the growing amalgamation of the two countries.

I come from the only region in the United States that is north of some parts of Canada—the area where the Underground operated so actively during the period of the emancipation. To the people of this region, "Uncle Tom" is as much a Canadian as he is a Southerner, and the bitter warfare on this border between our own sections was much more violent than anything that had torn us apart from Canada. . . .

Our other sense of Canada is that of a vacation land. It *is* a vacation land and I think if you were to poll the ordinary citizen in the United States, he would suggest to you that his concept of Canada is either that of a place where a very, very British group is trying to hang on to British accents and British designs, or of the picturesque French-Canadian rural countryside.

II. THE CONSERVATIVES COME TO POWER

EDITOR'S INTRODUCTION

The national victories of the Progressive-Conservatives in 1957 and 1958 made many Americans take a second, if not a first, look at Canada. The Liberals, in power for so many years, had been publicly identified as "pro-American"; the Conservatives, if not described as anti-American, nevertheless were viewed as less inclined to be friendly.

The introductory article supplies a brief sketch of the national political parties and their leaders. Next a report from the *Atlantic Monthly* attributes the Conservatives' victory to their ability to convert the anti-American overtones of a first narrow victory (1957) into "the 1958 pro-Canadianism which swept the entire nation." H. S. Ferns, in the article which follows, believes the real change came about when John Diefenbaker became head of the Conservative party. Diefenbaker succeeded because he was able to reach the people as a whole, the "outsiders," and thus Fern attributes the victory to a reaction against ministerial dictatorship, excessive bigness and international influences in Canadian life. In the final article there is a brief look at a minority party of "outsiders" which is a Canadian kin of the British Labour party. No longer a national party, it retains its local power in the western province of Saskatchewan.

CANADA'S PARTIES [1]

All Canadians twenty-one years of age and over, and eligible under universal franchise provisions, have the right to vote. . . . Canada follows the British system. Her election days come on

[1] From "Canada's Federal Election" by J. F. Mutchmor, Canadian correspondent. *Christian Century.* 74:680-1. May 29, 1957. Reprinted by permission.

the average every four years, but not at any set calendar time. Her prime minister and the other members of the federal cabinet are elected representatives of constituencies. There is not the clear-cut division of executive, legislative and judicial powers that obtains in the U.S.A. In Canada legislative and executive powers are combined, but the judicial ones are separate and strongly guarded.

Geographically, Canada is divided into five parts: the four Atlantic provinces, Quebec, Ontario, the three Prairie provinces, and British Columbia. Quebec with 75 seats is French Canadian. Ontario with 85 seats is its chiefly English-speaking counterpart. The Atlantic provinces have 33, the Prairies 48, and British Columbia 22 seats. Yukon and Mackenzie River each elect a member. The two central provinces have 160 of the 265 seats in the House of Commons.

Politically power is divided among two major and two minor parties. The two major ones are the Liberals and the Progressive-Conservatives, corresponding to quite an extent in principles and history to the Democrats and the Republicans in the U.S.A. . . . The two minor parties are the CCF (Canadian Commonwealth Federation) or Socialists, and the Social Crediters. There is a sprinkling of Communists banded together as the Labor Progressive party, but they have almost no political power. In a few constituencies they may be a nuisance.

The Liberal party . . . [during the election campaign of June 1957 which ended the twenty-two-year uninterrupted period in which the Liberals held power without a break was] headed by a French-Canadian lawyer, Louis St. Laurent, popularly called "Uncle Louis." This Liberal leader at the age of 75 . . . adds drive and vigor to his party's cause with all the vim of a man in his middle fifties. St. Laurent is a devoted and ardent Roman Catholic. This fact spells no liability, not even in the most Protestant constituency.

[After the Liberal defeat in June 1957 Lester B. ("Mike") Pearson was chosen to head the Liberal party. Pearson is well known inside and outside of Canada through his work in the United Nations. He served as Minister of External Affairs during

the tenure of the Liberals and received the Nobel Peace Prize in
1957.—Ed.]

Johnny Diefenbaker heads the Progressive-Conservative party.
He is a lone ranger from Saskatchewan, being the only representative of his group in that large province. Diefenbaker, a loyal
Baptist, also is a lawyer. He is a hard-driving, tireless campaigner,
an able debater and a strong and resourceful leader. . . .

M. J. Coldwell, a former schoolteacher, leads the Socialist
CCF. He also is from Saskatchewan. The premier of this
province is T. L. Douglas, the head of Canada's only Socialist
government. . . .

Finally, Solon Low, a Church of Latter Day Saints member, is
leader of the Social Crediters, whose voting strength is chiefly in
Alberta (counterpart of Texas) and British Columbia. The
SC's are not doctrinaire but rather realistic and conservative
people.

THE CONSERVATIVE LANDSLIDE [2]

The Conservative landslide in the Canadian election on
March 31 [1958] made history. Never before has a political
party been smitten so grievously as was the Liberal party under
its brand-new leader, Lester B. Pearson. The Conservative party
not only won 209 seats of a house of 265, it wiped out Liberal
representation in six of the country's ten provinces, including all
of western Canada. It got 53 per cent of the popular vote, to
the Liberals' 36 per cent. Indeed, the only parallel in modern
history was the Landon debacle in 1936.

Followers of Prime Minister John Diefenbaker cracked the
historic Liberal citadel of Quebec wide open. The Liberal
majority of 10,000 to 15,000 a year ago was transformed into
Conservative gains. The Conservatives obliterated the Social
Crediters in Alberta and British Columbia. The Liberal party,
which had a 163 to 57 margin over the Conservatives before the
June, 1957, election, was reduced to only 47 members. The once
cocky Socialist party, the Cooperative Commonwealth Federation,

[2] From "The Atlantic Report: Canada." *Atlantic Monthly.* 201:18-23. June
1958. Reprinted by permission.

saw all its top leaders beaten in what were regarded as the safest seats in the country and its strength cut from 25 to 8.

The bitterest taste for the so-called reform parties was the way in which the Conservatives won 16 out of 17 seats in Saskatchewan—where since 1944 the CCF has been in complete control—and took all 17 seats in Alberta, where the Social Credit monetary reformers have owned the provincial government since 1935. All this happened with whopping majorities in seats in which Conservative candidates usually ran last. And it happened quietly in an issue-free election in which the public seemed completely unconcerned.

For Pearson, who came fresh to the Liberal leadership from a distinguished career at the United Nations as Canada's top spokesman, it was a bitter blow. Yet the gathering disaster for the Liberals was apparent from the first days of the Liberal convention in Ottawa last January, at which Pearson was elected to succeed the Right Honorable Louis S. St. Laurent, Liberal leader and Prime Minister from 1948 to 1957.

Under Liberal administration, from 1935 to 1957, the country prospered mightily. Its population grew from 11 million to 16.5 million. Its trade expanded with the forced-draft development of Canadian industry. Liberal fiscal policies encouraged foreign investment, and American investment in Canada rose from a prewar $3 billion to $13 billion. As a direct result of this flow of capital northward, Canadian heavy industry, manufacturing, and natural resources development came substantially under U.S. ownership and control.

The Tide of Nationalism

Public reaction to the boom was reflected in easy Liberal victories at the polls. But the longer it lasted, the more convinced did the Liberals become that they had found the secret of eternal power. They became arrogant in office. They let political fences decay. The Liberal administration did what was "good for the country" and not what was politically beneficial. It antagonized old-age pensioners with picayune pension increases, it distributed tax reductions with bad grace, it was timid in protesting to Washington against trade policies that hurt Canadian farmers.

Its engineers, not party politicians, dictated policy on public works.

Above all, the Liberals ignored the tide of nationalism that was slowly but surely rising in Canada. They seemed to be more concerned with the United Nations than with pressing Canadian problems.

During their twenty-two years in the wilderness, the Conservatives saw many seemingly potent issues collapse in their hands. They tried leader after leader with little success. Through a process of elimination they ran through an imposing list and came to John Diefenbaker, an able 62-year-old lawyer from Saskatchewan, who captured the leadership of the party in 1957. . . .

In the campaign that followed, there were no real issues. There was only a quiet but growing Canadian nationalism, which has become apparent since the American ownership of so large a share of Canadian industry was brought out into the open. In the June, 1957, election campaign, this was closely akin to anti-Americanism. All the best issues which the Conservatives seized upon had strong American coloration. It was from this fact, and Diefenbaker's expressed aim of diverting 15 per cent of Canada's imports from the United States to Britain, that the Liberals drew their main texts at their January convention.

The Conservatives, they said, had created unemployment by destroying American confidence in Canada. If Canada was the best U.S. customer, the United States was Canada's best customer, too. Each was important to the other, and ill will was a luxury neither could afford. "We put it very simply," Pearson said after his leadership victory in January. "We think we know how to get along with the Americans, and the Conservatives do not."

The Liberals sought to use an American "slap down" at Canada, in Commerce Secretary Weeks's phrase, as a club with which to belabor the Tories. They tried to sell the obviously preposterous notion that the U.S. imposition of a 15 per cent import reduction on Canadian oil was in retaliation for Diefenbaker's proposal that 15 per cent of Canada's imports be diverted to the Commonwealth from the United States. The strategy backfired.

The Conservatives, in this campaign, successfully converted the anti-American overtones of the 1957 campaign into the 1958 pro-Canadianism which swept the entire nation. Diefenbaker said out loud what many Canadians have felt. He not only preached the building of a Canadian New Jerusalem, he launched a great public works program to get it started. In the Maritime provinces he poured money into the financing of steam power plants to breathe some life into a dying coal industry. In Ontario he dwelt upon the necessity of using Canadian raw materials in Canada to manufacture goods for Canadian use and raise Canada's standard of living. In the west he gave the go-ahead to the long controversial $250 million Saskatchewan River dam for power and irrigation. He outlined plans for pushing back frontiers and opening up the north. He appointed a Royal Energy Commission to develop a national energy use policy. . . .

Election Promises

The Liberal campaign became a futile search for a glamorous formula that would catch the attention of the Canadian electorate. The attempt to capitalize on Canadian friendship with the United States blew up when it put the Liberals in the position of being allied with Americans against Canadian Conservatives.

Pearson [the Liberal party leader] proposed a multimillion dollar program of scholarships for university students. That was a dud. He came out for income tax exemptions for young people during their first two years of marriage. He proposed various cuts in taxation which were complicated enough to alienate even the chartered accountant vote. He proposed an equally complicated agricultural policy that impressed farmers only with its impracticality. Yet even proposals which attracted attention were rendered harmless by a single Tory question: "They promise it now, but they voted against it last year. Why didn't they do it when they were in power?"

The Conservatives, in eight months, could point to a long list of election promises fulfilled. They had raised the old-age pensions; they got a study going of the United States Social Security Act, pumped money into the Maritimes, enacted floor price legislation, extended unemployment insurance. These token payments, as it were, convinced thousands of uncommitted Canadians that Diefenbaker's party was entitled to "see what it can do with a working majority." This, coupled with Diefenbaker's basic appeal to Canadian nationalism, gave the Conservatives the greatest parliamentary strength in Canadian history. How will that strength be used?

After the election, Canadian second thoughts were that the victory had been too one-sided, that a better result would have been a Conservative win by a narrow margin. On the other hand, it is gradually dawning on people that there is more to this election result than mere numbers. Almost since confederation in 1867, Canada has been ruled by the bloc which has been able to attract the most outside support. The Liberals had the solid French-Canadian bloc from Quebec. The Conservatives had a solid English-Canadian bloc from Ontario. Under Canada's system a responsible government power resides in the caucus of the government party, not on the floor of Parliament. The cabinet must always obtain the support of its members in caucus before it takes its measures before Parliament.

Despite the debate in the House of Commons, enactment of government measures is certain. When the caucus was dominated by either of the blocs, the influence of less populous areas diminished. That was accentuated when regional discontent sent minority parties to Parliament from Saskatchewan, Alberta, and British Columbia. These provinces went largely unrepresented in government caucus for many years.

This year, Ontario elected 68 Conservatives, the four western provinces and the northern territories 66, Quebec elected 50, and the Maritimes 25. Thus no one region, no one interest, and no one racial group can dominate the others. Greater protection will be extended to Canadian industry, as Ontario demands, but it will have to be done in such a way that it does not raise a storm in western Canada and in the Maritimes.

A NEW COURSE IN CANADIAN POLITICS? [3]

After twenty-two years of uninterrupted power the Liberal party of Canada has suddenly lost its commanding position in Canadian affairs. A year ago students of Canadian politics were still baffled by the apparently undiminished trend towards one-party dominance of the federal government of Canada. Now that trend has been dramatically broken off. . . .

If we admit that in the politics of Canada there is much that is mysterious and much that eludes explanation, we can none the less attempt some illumination. We are obliged first to reject the materialist, economic interpretation of Canadian politics which has come to underlie much Liberal thinking about Canadian affairs; the assumption that material prosperity solves all problems; the assumption summed up in the complacent Liberal proposition that "nobody's going to shoot Santa Claus." Instead we are obliged to accept the more difficult and older assumption that in Canadian politics less tangible factors than the gross national income still have a significance; factors like religion, conceptions of the meaning of life, and racial and cultural inheritances. . . .

It is now possible to argue that the real change in Canadian politics came about when the present Prime Minister, Mr. J. G. Diefenbaker, displaced Mr. George Drew as leader of the Conservative party [in 1956]. Mr. Drew is what an Englishman would recognize as a man of the Establishment: wealthy and connected with wealth, wealthily educated; privately a man of some cultivation, but in his public personality, arrogant, obscurantist, and extreme. Enjoying considerable support in his native province of Ontario, Mr. Drew believed that he could win power in Canada by arranging cooperation between himself and the leading political personalities of the clerical-reactionary [provincial] party of Quebec, the *Union Nationale* of Maurice Duplessis. It can be said on Mr. Drew's behalf that he had realistically assumed the character of the Canadian Establishment

[3] From "The New Course in Canadian Politics," article by H. S. Ferns, senior lecturer in modern history and government, the University of Birmingham in England, coauthor of *The Age of Mackenzie King*, and formerly a member of the secretarial staff of the Prime Minister of Canada. *Political Quarterly*. 29:114-23. April-June 1958. Reprinted by permission.

and that he understood very well the dual character of the Canadian powerhouse comprised as it is of business wealth and clerical power. Mr. Drew inadequately appreciated, however, the ambivalent attitude of Canadians of all classes and racial origins to both wealth and clerical power. Canadians very generally love money and love God, but they are not unqualified admirers of entrenched men of wealth nor of cardinals, archbishops, and the practitioners of organized religion. . . .

Mr. Diefenbaker is quite a different type of politician to Mr. Drew. He is an outsider; the first genuine outsider to achieve high office in Canada since . . . 1911. . . . Mr. Diefenbaker has always been a man in a minority; a man with a non-Anglo-Saxon name in a predominantly Anglo-Saxon party; a Conservative in the predominantly Liberal or Socialist [Cooperative Commonwealth Federation] province of Saskatchewan; a lawyer in a small prairie town far away from the centers of big business; a Baptist in a country where the powerful people belong either to the Roman Catholic Church or to the Protestant United Church of Canada; a man with a law degree from a prairie college in a nation where leading bureaucrats are graduates of Oxford, Cambridge, Harvard, Columbia, Chicago, and Toronto.

When Mr. Diefenbaker was elected leader of the Conservative party, the Quebec Conservatives connected with Duplessis walked out of the Convention. Instead of submitting to bullying of this kind, Mr. Diefenbaker abandoned completely the tactics of Mr. Drew. . . . During the election campaign Mr. Diefenbaker made no attempt to win Quebec. He made only three speeches in that province, and these short ones. . . .

Mr. Diefenbaker's electoral campaign was directed to the people as a whole. Apart from Quebec, he made it his object to see and speak personally to as many people as possible. Never since the days of Laurier [Wilfrid Laurier, Prime Minister 1896-1911] has Canada witnessed such a close personal approach to the people by a national political leader as that established by Mr. Diefenbaker. The outsider went to the outsiders, and as the results show, he got their votes.

In his grass roots campaign Mr. Diefenbaker stressed two simple themes: the need for Canadian independence of the United States and the need to rescue parliamentary government in Canada from ministerial dictatorship. In his discussion of Canadian-American relations Mr. Diefenbaker was never stridently anti-American. No Canadian in his right mind wants bad relations with the United States, but many—a majority—believe that "dependency upon the United States has gone too far, that Canadian well-being, the Canadian economy, are far too vulnerable to American whims and American reversals." This is not emotional rhetoric. It sums up a variety of anxieties in Canadian minds, both material and spiritual. Canadian farmers are affected by American competitive methods in the world grain market. Canadian industrial interests—both employers and employees—are affected by the growing shortages of electric power caused in part by the enormous use of electric power by processing industries supplying raw and semi-processed materials like aluminum and newsprint to the American market. The prospect of industrial expansion in British Columbia depends upon how hydroelectric power is developed in that province and how it is distributed. If a high proportion of hydroelectric energy generated on the upper reaches of the Columbia River is sold to the industrial complex of Washington and Oregon, industry in British Columbia—at least in the southern areas where most people now live—will soon have reached its limits. Similar questions surround the use of oil and gas resources. Above and beyond this question is the wisdom of putting all the Canadian economic eggs in the American basket. If a slump hits the United States Canada will be affected more seriously than any nation on earth.

The relations of Canadian industry with American industry are no longer beset primarily by the fear of a small-scale industry threatened by the competitive powers of large-scale American industry. In some lines Canadian manufacturers can undersell American manufacturers in the American market. The issue now concerns much more the use of power and raw material resources.

One of the great themes of Canadian experience has been resistance to the United States. Until after the American Civil War, while the United States was a rapidly expanding land

empire, this threat was of a military character. Such is no longer
the case. The American threat to Canadian existence is now
economic, cultural, and political. Canada came into being as a
reaction to the American Revolution, and part of Canada's character has been formed in reacting against American influences.
Some argue that, whether Canadians like it or not, they are
bound to become American in their culture, politics, and religious sentiments just as they are bound to be integrated in the
American economy. The Roman Catholic, French-Canadian part
of Canada has offered stubborn resistance to "North Americani-
zation" on the cultural and religious level, but rather less resistance on the economic level, even inviting economic penetration
with assurances that greater social stability and less "labor trouble"
prevail in Quebec than elsewhere. The Protestant English-
speaking parts of Canada offer less resistance to American
spiritual influences, and the same can be said of most immigrant
groups, but these parts of the Canadian community contain a
high percentage of people in all classes who are "economically
minded" and for them the hard material facts of Canadian-
American relations are important and formative influences in
their political reactions. Whether they are farmers, wage workers, employers, or investors, none of these powerful interest
groups can entertain a simple, uncritical attitude to the United
States any more than can the bishops of Quebec fighting to protect their followers from what they conceive to be a multitude
of secular evils of American inspiration. These are some of the
reasons why American-Canadian relations have never been, and
cannot be, wrapped up in rhetoric about an undefended frontier
and a common front against dictatorship, and then forgotten.
The Conservative victory in Canada has underlined this fact once
again, and the Liberals have been beaten partly because they had
forgotten it.

Mr. Diefenbaker's second theme during his electoral campaign concerned the ministerial domination of Parliament and
the progressive attenuation of the authority of the House of
Commons during the Liberal regime. The most recent manifestations of this tendency have consisted of the use of the closure
in debate and the scandalous partisanship of the Speaker during

the last Parliament. The trouble is, however, much deeper than this, and it may fairly be said that the Conservatives themselves have not made a very convincing analysis of what has happened to the structure of Canadian politics during the long predominance of the Liberal party. . . .

An expert bureaucracy has grown up in Ottawa connected with the central bank, the diplomatic service, the treasury, the welfare services, the armed forces, and the scientific research establishments. For many years the way to the highest public honors has not been, as it was until 1914, through the constituencies and the House of Commons but through the civil service. Mr. Mackenzie King [Liberal Prime Minister, 1921-1930, 1935-1948] commenced his career in the civil service, and never showed during his long political life any capacity to get himself elected in a constituency. For most of his career he sat for pocket boroughs belonging to the Liberal party. His successor, Mr. St. Laurent, was invited into politics late in life, and presented with a seat in the House of Commons. . . . Indeed, an atmosphere had developed in Ottawa in which election to Parliament was the least of a man's qualifications for office, while affiliation to the powerhouse of the bureaucracy was indispensable to progress in a political career. . . . The way to high office wound through the corridors of the East Block [of the Parliament Building which houses much of the Civil Service] and the Bank of Canada, and not so very often through the smoking rooms of the Parliament. The House of Commons and the constituencies were late not early phases of a career, and the man who started in a constituency and who relied on that fact alone was bound to end up like a rural squire sitting for a county in the days of Lord North. . . . The process of forty years' duration has now been arrested—at least momentarily, and the elected part of the machinery of government in Canada has once more come into its own. . . .

While it is possible to expect something new of Mr. Diefenbaker's leadership, it is unlikely, and certainly not part of his design, to alter in any fundamental way the structure of Canadian authority. Now that he has power, he will inevitably be drawn, as all new Canadian governments have been drawn, into adjusting himself, his ideas, and his party to the requirements of the dominant organizations of the community. It is popularly supposed that the Canadian Conservative party is a party of "big business" and that, of course, there can be no problem of adjustment with the major business groups. Recent research has, however, revealed that the Conservative party has not always served the interests of the most powerful sections of the business class. . . . My own researches have demonstrated the connection of the Liberals with "big business," particularly American "big business." Indeed, it is a fair inference from such facts as are known that the Conservative party is much more closely connected with the middle ranges of business than with the most powerful concentrations of financial power in Canada and in the United States. What adjustment Mr. Diefenbaker will make with these powerful groups is difficult to determine. If he acts primarily to please his supporters, we may expect him to strengthen Canadian control over power and raw material resources and to canalize the flow of capital more into final manufactures than has been the case during the last twenty years. We can expect him, too, to take a more aggressive line in promoting the sale of Canadian agricultural and industrial products abroad, particularly in the Caribbean, Africa, and the Far East.

Politically Mr. Diefenbaker's most important problem is Quebec and his relations with the Roman Catholic Church. Thus far in Canadian history every government, no matter how Protestant or anticlerical its first thoughts were, has felt obliged to come to terms with the French-speaking part of the Roman Catholic Church. Mr. Diefenbaker is more cut off from this source of power than any major political leader in Canadian history. This being so, it will be extremely interesting to see how he will solve this problem. . . .

Canada has always been since the American Revolution a plural society, and the seeds of death begin to sprout in any political movement which forgets this fact. This has been conspicuously the case of the Liberal party. It had allowed itself too completely to become the party of "big business" and "big church."

The plural character of Canadian society is the baffling problem of every Canadian political party; and always more baffling to the party in power than the parties in opposition. Big business and ecclesiastical organizations with their international affiliations are indispensable factors in Canadian life; inescapable consequences of geographical and historical circumstances. In spite of this, the Canadian community is constantly generating groups which are small and locally centered. These groups are moved by fear and envy of the big, old, and well-established organizations, and they feel constantly the impulse to grow and seek their own place in the sun. As a result newer and/or smaller interests find very congenial political provincialism and nationalism offering on the domestic plane opposition to big government in Ottawa and on the international plane presenting a critical face towards the great powers or institutions most intimately connected with Canadian life. Protestant groups, locally centered and individualist, have concentrated on opposition to Rome. The xenophobia once directed mainly towards London is now focused on the United States.

No moderately sane and sensitive Canadian objects to "big business" and "big church" or fails to recognize their necessity, and the advantages of Canada's intimate connections in Washington, London, and Rome. But there can be too much of a good thing. The Conservative victory was a reaction against bigness and international influences in Canadian life. But this argument must not be pressed too far. The Conservative reaction was against an excess and not against big organizations and foreign influences *in toto*. The pluralism of the Liberal party had become unreal. The pluralism of the Conservative party is at the moment real, and is likely to remain so for many years, gradually becoming false as it remains in office. . . .

Whether the Liberal party will ever recover . . . is doubtful. The future belongs to the Conservative party as the political instrument of the established interests, and the next phase of Canadian history will be concerned largely with the establishment of this instrumentality. The future belongs, too, to the Cooperative Commonwealth Federation as the party of the outsiders. What little social idealism there is in Canadian society has become concentrated in this party. Liberal in sentiment as the Conservative party is at the moment, the Cooperative Commonwealth Federation is much more so. In the present condition of prosperity in Canada there are few really poor people, but there are many who are exploited and driven hard by the economy. Even more are outsiders. This is particularly true of societies embracing large numbers of immigrants, and Canada presents an archetype of such a society.

A PARTY OF OUTSIDERS [4]

The CCF [Cooperative Commonwealth Federation] was formed at a conference of farm, labor and socialist organizations held in Calgary [Alberta] in August, 1932, and its first program was drawn up at a convention held in Regina [Saskatchewan] in 1933.

Behind these two conferences lay a long history of protest movements in Canada, including a great wave of protest which swept the nation immediately after World War I and manifested itself in the Winnipeg General Strike of 1919, in the election of farmer governments in Ontario, Alberta and Manitoba, and in the victory of 65 farmer candidates (called "Progressives") in the federal general election of 1921. Unfortunately, these protest movements had neither effective organization nor a clear idea of how to remove the causes of their discontent; so they petered out.

Even so, the desire for fundamental social change persisted and found expression in various organizations across the country. It became apparent also in the House of Commons in the 1920's, where a few of the more determined Progressives began to cooperate with a small labor group. Out of this partnership there developed a spirited opposition force known as the "Ginger Group."

Slowly the idea emerged that a welter of unconnected organizations and a mere informal group in the House of Commons

---

[4] From *What Is The CCF?*, pamphlet by Ken Bryden, formerly Deputy Minister of Labor in Saskatchewan. Cooperative Commonwealth Federation. Ottawa, Ontario. 1952. [no pagination].

were not enough. What was needed was one coordinated political movement. Patient negotiations were carried on to form such
a movement.

Just as these negotiations were reaching fruition another important event occurred with the formation in January, 1932, of
the League for Social Reconstruction. This brought together in
one organization two groups of Montreal and Toronto scholars
who had been studying the social, political and economic situation in Canada and had come to the conclusion that democratic
socialism offered the only real answer to the nation's problems.

The upshot of all these developments was the Calgary conference of 1932. The organizations represented at Calgary varied
in background and outlook but the impelling need to form a
movement greater than any of them led them to submerge differences of approach and to unite in the CCF.

The CCF differed from the protest movements of the past in
two fundamental ways. First, by pooling their resources, the
groups that founded it provided a basis on which effective organization could be built. Second, the research work of the League
for Social Reconstruction made it possible from the beginning
to develop a rounded statement of principles and a practical
program of action.

CCF stands for Cooperative Commonwealth Federation. This
was the name chosen by the delegates at the Calgary conference
from among many proposed to them.

The new organization was called a federation because at the
time it was exactly that—a federation of the various organizations represented at Calgary.

The words "Cooperative Commonwealth" in the name indicate the basic objective of the movement. To quote the first
program, the aim of the CCF "is the establishment in Canada
of a Cooperative Commonwealth in which the principle regulat-
ing production, distribution and exchange will be the supplying
of human needs and not the making of profits." . . .

The CCF . . . believes in gradually and democratically replacing the present capitalist system with a cooperative society in
which men and women will work together to solve their common
problems. . . .

The democratic socialist philosophy of the CCF is the opposite of communism.

Communists aim at building a small but highly trained and disciplined group who will mastermind a revolution and then will establish a dictatorship to protect and extend the revolution. Anything goes if they think it will promote, protect or extend the revolution. The most deceitful maneuverings and the most blatant brutality are not only regarded as legitimate but take on the character almost of a sacred crusade.

The CCF rejects this vicious philosophy absolutely. It denies that good can come from the suppression of human beings in a dictatorship. It affirms that a better society can be built by the slow and sure method of constitutional change, in which the individual is at all times exalted and given steadily increasing opportunity to lead the good life. . . .

The CCF consists of (a) individual members who are organized in clubs and constituency associations, and (b) trade unions and other economic and cultural organizations which have been accepted as affiliates. The government of the CCF is entirely in the hands of these individual members and affiliated organizations.

Because Canada has a federal system of government, the CCF has both national and provincial organizations. . . . In only a little more than twenty years it has become well established as the government of one province (Saskatchewan), it has elected members to the legislatures of most other provinces and is the official opposition in some provinces.

In the federal House of Commons it has an able group who are regarded by most independent observers as the real opposition to the government.

Moreover, the CCF, even though not in office, has had a profound effect on Canadian life. Few will deny that its constant campaigning, reinforced by the election of CCF candidates, has been a major factor in forcing reluctant old party governments to adopt such measures as unemployment insurance, family allowances and old age pensions.

III. CANADA, THE COMMONWEALTH AND THE WORLD

EDITOR'S INTRODUCTION

Canada has, particularly since World War II, become increasingly aware of its role in world affairs. As noted in Section II foreign policy has become an important matter for internal debate and a determinant of political fortunes. The articles in this section deal with Canada's political ties with the British Commonwealth, its ties to the United States, and its emergence as a "middle power" in an era of political giants.

The first four articles deal with Canada's role in world affairs and the nature of its bonds with the Commonwealth. In the first selection Lester B. Pearson, head of the Liberal party, says that Canadian acceptance of the British Crown is based on more than sentiment or historical caprice; the British system of parliamentary government, represented by the Crown, gives a sense of continuity to Canadian history and is a stabilizing force in Canadian national development. Neil McKenty next reviews Canadian foreign policy, tracing the evolution from isolation and neutrality in world affairs through active cooperation in World War II to the recent assumption of an independent role as a leading member of the United Nations. The third selection argues that Canada as a "particularly favorably situated" middle power can play an influential role as a mediator among the great powers if it exercises a "sane statesmanship." The fourth author, Robert A. Spencer, assesses the effect of the Conservative victory upon foreign policy. After reviewing the initial actions of the Diefenbaker government, Mr. Spencer stresses the necessary continuity of policy and concludes that any change in this area will be negligible.

The following selections emphasize the ties between the United States and Canada: what strains them and what makes them endure. Raymond Daniell, correspondent for the New

York *Times,* points out that the peaceful frontier is no accident: a major factor in the smooth flow of relations has been the legal arrangements made for use and diversion of the boundary waters. Whatever differences Canada and the United States may have with each other, according to the next selection, economic necessity and common defense needs make their close collaboration imperative. In two further selections, the reader is introduced to a dramatic instance of close collaboration: the erection and maintenance of the Distant Early Warning line which guards the North American continent against surprise air attack.

The last four articles discuss areas of tension which have at times strained relations between the two nations. The first two describe these as: (1) the tariff problem; (2) commercial rivalry; (3) differences in matters of global policy; and (4) disagreement on how to deal with subversion. In an interview which follows the Prime Minister of Canada talks about economic relations between the two countries: Canadians, he says, don't want their economic affairs determined outside Canada but Canada needs the United States and the United States needs Canada. In the final article, a Canadian scholar speaks out against the "current anti-Americanism" in Canada. "Whether we like the situation or not," he concludes, "some of the strongest influences on Canadian life and thought are American." Thus he admonishes his countrymen that understanding and evaluation, not outraged protest against these influences, will help Canada to grow in maturity as a nation.

THE CROWN AND THE COMMONWEALTH [1]

I would like to speak to you . . . of . . . [a] world-wide association known as the Commonwealth of Nations—the importance of which should never be underestimated in adding up the resources on the side of the free world. Here by the shores of the Pacific, it seems to me appropriate that we should

[1] From address by Lester B. Pearson, then Canadian Secretary of State for External Affairs, delivered at the University of Oregon, Eugene, May 25, 1953. Mimeographed text supplied by the Information Division, Department of External Affairs, Ottawa, Ontario.

examine together the new forces at work in the Commonwealth, which in its modern form, now bridges the East and West.

This Commonwealth of Nations is a group of eight independent and sovereign countries, linked together by the Crown, by past cooperation, by unifying traditions and, even more important now, by a common devotion to freedom. It contains also a large number of dependent territories, nearly all of them linked to the United Kingdom—and all themselves progressing toward complete freedom and self-government, which must be accepted as the ultimate goal of every colonial people.

These independent but associated countries with their dependent territories are to be found in every continent and cover about one fifth of the land surface of the globe. Their total population, including people of many different races, colors and creeds, is more than 600 million; close to one quarter of the inhabitants of the world. . . .

Our acceptance of the Crown as a symbol of this association was based on more than sentiment or on loyalty of the heart. There was this, certainly, particularly among those whose personal histories were not far removed from the British Isles; but there was a great deal more. There was also a conviction that the Crown had a unifying and stabilizing value in our national growth. For countries such as Australia, New Zealand and Canada, the Crown stood not for tyranny but for the British system of parliamentary government, painfully and slowly wrought since the days of Magna Carta. We desired to preserve this for our own use and adapt it to fit our own needs. It represented the continuity of our history and gave depth and solidity to our development. Today we feel in Canada that the Crown—in the person of our gracious and lovely Queen—lends order and dignity to our national life, standing, as it does, above the play of party controversies. We think it is good to be able to honor the head of state—and berate the head of government—at one and the same time. You, whose distant political origins were identical with ours, have created your own system of popular government which has exerted such a profound influence on the development of democratic institutions throughout the world. But the Commonwealth countries, while adhering—

with one exception—more closely to the older forms, have achieved an independence and a distinct character no less real and complete than others; a fact which I find is sometimes not understood in the United States.

Our Queen, who wears the Crown, is the monarch of several nations, each "in no way subordinate one to the other." It is true that it is the Queen of the United Kingdom who is also the Queen of Canada. That, however, is a result of our past history, which the people of Canada gladly accept of their own free will.

In Canada the Queen is represented by a Governor General, who, incidentally and to make matters more confusing to outsiders, is not a general and does not govern. The present Governor General is a distinguished Canadian for whom we have deep respect, and who was the first Canadian diplomatic representative to the United States.

The Queen will shortly proclaim for use in Canada a Royal Style and Title chosen and approved by the Parliament of Canada, and she will do the same for each Commonwealth country which recognizes her as Queen, using the styles and titles desired by the parliament of those countries. One title, which will be used by all, however, is "Head of the Commonwealth." This is because India which is a republic and has a president as head of state, recognizes the Queen simply as Head of the Commonwealth. . . .

At times the idea of the Commonwealth is a puzzling and difficult one for people outside it—and even some inside it— to grasp. Some time ago, I read in an American publication an article entitled "The Commonwealth Cult—What Really Binds Britain and the Dominions." In this article the author says with some cynicism:

The Commonwealth appears in fact to be no more than an alumni association without an executive committee, bylaws or a program of concerted action whose individual, spirited, self-willed members, presided over by their former headmaster, recognize no other obligations towards one another than may be prompted by the heart or by considerations of far-sighted self-interest.

In another publication (this time a British one) I have seen the Commonwealth described in even more critical terms:

A sprawling collection of nations with no common obligations, with no coordinated line of action in world affairs and at odds with each other, make up an international system which is a travesty of the word "Commonwealth."

What these authors have *failed* to do is to distinguish sufficiently between form and substance. Yet this distinction lies at the root of an understanding of the Commonwealth. This elastic and adaptable association has weathered many storms, and has in the past proved its vigor and usefulness, not only to its own members, but to the world, by its remarkable capacity for meeting and dealing with practical situations; and for altering its outward forms to meet new problems as they arise. It may well face even more difficult tests in the future. I hope it will meet them successfully because this association has, I think, importance and value for more than its members.

So far, in spite of its anomalies, the Commonwealth has worked. . . .

Most Canadians would say that the central reason why the Commonwealth persists (despite occasional gloomy predictions that its days are numbered) is due as much as anything to the absence of formal and binding central machinery, and to the flexibility and freedom of its working arrangements. The Commonwealth has, for instance, no common legislation, no binding defense agreements, no Chiefs of Staff Committee, no common tariff structure, no central foreign office.

There seems to be a good deal of perplexity in other countries about this absence of central institutions—of "organization." We feel, however, that everything that it is possible to do through the Commonwealth, can be done without such formal, rigid institutions, which might prejudice the freedom of the separate parts. It is the consensus of Commonwealth opinion that the conduct of each member's own affairs would be made more difficult—if not quite impossible—if such formal institutions existed; and that this, in its turn, would make a free and cooperative association difficult to maintain.

The Commonwealth has shown in the past—and is showing today—that—notwithstanding its informal, almost casual structure—it is an association capable of contributing in no small measure to the strength and stability of the free world.

A BRIEF RÉSUMÉ OF FOREIGN POLICY [2]

During the last quarter of the nineteenth century . . . [Canada's] objectives were simple: to prevent absorption by her gigantic southern neighbor, and to gain increased control over her own affairs within the British Empire. Canada had few relations with other countries during this period. She was too busy trying to survive, trapped (as she thought) between United States imperialism and British diplomacy.

Canada's first Prime Minister, Sir John A. Macdonald, considered the price he had to pay at the 1871 Washington Conference (fishing rights and San Juan Islands) far too high for the dubious honor of being the first Canadian to sign an international treaty. Again, at the turn of the century, Canadian interests were squeezed between "Manifest Destiny" and British compromise when England supported the American claims to the Alaskan "panhandle."

The British connection itself posed a thorny problem for Canada. She had no voice in the formulation of British foreign policy, but was none the less expected to fight in Britain's wars. This inequity was further complicated by cultural divisions within Canada herself. English imperialists, particularly in Ontario, were "ready, aye, ready" to support any British action at the drop of a hat. Isolationist groups, concentrated in Quebec, were all for staying at home whenever Canada's own interests were not directly involved.

French-Catholic Prime Minister Sir Wilfrid Laurier (1896-1911) gingerly steered a middle course between the two groups by admitting that any British declaration of war legally committed Canada, but that the latter would determine the extent

[2] From "Canada's New Stature," by Neil McKenty, S.J., a student of theology at Jesuit Seminary, Toronto, Ontario. *America.* 97:226-8. May 18, 1957. Reprinted from *America* (America Press, New York 17, N.Y.)

of her aid. Again and again Laurier insisted that Canada would not be bound in advance by a British foreign policy over which she had no control. "If you want our aid, call us to your councils," he bluntly told the British Government.

With increasing frequency during World War I and the peace negotiations, Canada was summoned to Britain's councils. When she insisted on and won an independent seat in the League of Nations, the Dominion became a nation in her own right. But if Canada had won the legal status of nationhood within the emerging Commonwealth, she was not yet ready to assume the international obligations which this position entailed. Isolationism was a safe and popular shibboleth between the wars; and Canada, for all practical purposes, adopted it enthusiastically.

When a Canadian official at the League stepped out of line by proposing oil sanctions against the aggressor after Italy attacked Ethiopia, the startled Canadian Government acted swiftly to pull the rug out from under him and to return to its official neutrality. Prime Minister Mackenzie King epitomized this policy when he told Parliament it was monstrous to think that Canada should risk the lives of her people every twenty years to help save a Europe that couldn't run itself.

World War II pricked the isolationist bubble once and for all. Having proved her right to an independent declaration of war by entering the hostilities a full week after England, Canada proceeded to make a splendid contribution of manpower and materials to the United Nations' cause. By so doing she became, in Churchill's phrase, "the linchpin" between Britain and the United States.

Just prior to the war, Canada had drawn closer to the United States. This was due in no little measure to President Franklin D. Roosevelt's frequent warm references to the Dominion, culminating in the President's assurance, made at Kingston, Ontario, in 1938, that his country would not stand idly by were her neighbor attacked. A few days later Mackenzie King promised reciprocity of defense. Canada fulfilled that pledge three years later when she became the first of all the Western nations to declare war on Japan.

By the end of the war, Canada had clearly emerged from the stage where her foreign policy consisted of a sheaf of non-committal platitudes tucked in the Prime Minister's desk. Shortly after Louis S. St. Laurent was appointed, in 1946, the first full-time Secretary of State for External Affairs, he laid down as one of the bases of Canadian foreign policy a "willingness to accept international responsibilities." Those responsibilities have come thick and fast during the past decade. Thanks to two superb foreign ministers, Mr. St. Laurent and Mr. Pearson, to a young but extremely able civil service and to an increasing maturity in public opinion about the vital issues at stake, Canada has measured up to her new responsibilities surprisingly well.

To Mr. St. Laurent himself is due a fair share of credit for the conception of the North Atlantic Treaty Organization. Canada, while emphasizing NATO's economic potential, has also backed the alliance with troops and air squadrons in Europe. A Canadian brigade fought in the Korean war and she is represented on the Indo-China armistice commission.

From the beginning, Canada has done her level best to make a workable body out of the UN, where Mr. Pearson spent a year as President of the General Assembly. . . .

Besides annual contributions to various UN agencies, the Government also supports the Colombo Plan, a Commonwealth assistance program for undeveloped countries. When the Hungarian refugee problem broke, Canadian immigration officials flew to Vienna, slashed through red tape, speeded up transportation facilities, and expect to have 25,000 Hungarians settled in the country by early summer.

If the Hungarian crisis provided an outlet for Canada's generosity, the Suez affair [which developed in July 1956 upon Egypt's nationalization of the Canal and lasted until November when hostilities between Egypt and Anglo-French-Israeli forces ended with acceptance of UN cease-fire proposal] marked a crucial development in her foreign policy. Almost overnight Canada was forced into a position of leadership and responsibility quite beyond anything she had attempted before. Her agonizing decision to break with her history by not supporting the United Kingdom in the Egyptian venture, and her subsequent sponsoring of a United Nations' police force commanded by a Canadian and containing numerous Canadian personnel, have placed this country and her leaders in the forefront of the "middle powers."

WHAT IS A MIDDLE POWER? [3]

Canada's development during the past two decades has been very much like that of the mushrooming adolescent. We've grown so big so quickly as the result of the Second World War that at the end of it we weren't at all sure just where we stood in relation to the other world powers. It was clearly no longer true to say that we were just a small power. On the other hand we were certainly not a great power. We thought of ourselves, then, as a middle power. But just how much weight has a middle power to throw around these days? How much influence does it or can it command? Can a middle power aspire to an independent foreign policy? And has Canada, as a middle power, such a policy? . . .

If by an independent foreign policy is meant one in the shaping of which the government enjoys an entirely free hand, then Canada hasn't such a policy. But then no state has. No foreign policy is wholly independent in this sense. Or (to paraphrase George Orwell) all foreign policies are dependent, but some are less dependent than others. . . .

Those who charge that Canadian foreign policy is lacking in independence may have one or more of a number of things in mind. They may feel that the Canadian economy hinders Canada's freedom of action in the field of foreign policy. They may think that the necessity for any Canadian government to carry, or at least not to alienate, Quebec may curtail the flexibility of foreign policy. They may think that Canada's traditional connection with the United Kingdom, or her membership in the Commonwealth, or both, tie her hands in world affairs. Or—

[3] From *Has Canada an Independent Foreign Policy?* pamphlet prepared by Canadian Association for Adult Education to accompany the Citizens' Forum broadcast on the same topic, February 1957. (Citizens' Forum pamphlet no 14) The Association. 113 St. George Street. Toronto 5, Ontario. 1957. Reprinted by permission.

perhaps the most common grievance today—it is felt that the United States, our huge neighbor so much more powerful than ourselves, calls the tune and we dance. There are other limitations, real or imagined, but perhaps these are the most frequently expressed and therefore the most important. Let's examine each in turn.

Are We Governed by Economic Needs?

There can be no gainsaying the fact that the Canadian economy is dependent on foreign markets for disposing of the staple commodities which it produces—wheat, timber, newsprint, minerals and so on. Failure to sell these in foreign markets would hit us all pretty hard. This fact is capable of limiting our foreign policy. . . .

As our domestic market expands, as our own economy is diversified, as more foreign markets are opened up, and as we discover and perfect ways of ironing out the kinks in the business cycle, this economic factor limiting our freedom of choice in foreign affairs is becoming less and less important. Today it is probably of little real significance.

A good illustration of its declining importance is to be found in our negotiations with the Soviet Union in the fall and winter of 1955-1956. The Russians' main objective in these negotiations was not to buy our wheat or to sell us furs. They wanted to get us to remove from the embargo which we had imposed during the Korean War certain strategic materials. They wanted us to do this partly because the materials would be useful to them, but mainly because such an action would have dismayed the United States and placed a strain upon Canadian-American relations. The Russian negotiators offered all kinds of inducements, but they were told plainly that there would be no deal. And there wasn't.

Foreign Policy and Our Two Cultures

There is a second kind of domestic limitation upon the independence of Canadian foreign policy. It is usually referred to as the necessity of maintaining our national unity—which is a politician's way of saying that the policy must command the

support of French-speaking Canadians. A government which for
any length of time on any major matter does not acquire at least
the acquiescence of the voters of the Province of Quebec is not
likely to remain the government. If anything can be said to be
a law of Canadian politics, this can. What, then, does it mean
for foreign policy?

The classic example of Canada's cultural complexity limiting
her freedom of action in the sphere of foreign affairs is . . . to
be found in the history of the 1930's. In 1935, the Canadian
permanent delegate at the League of Nations, finding himself
without definite instructions after a general election in the
Dominion, acted on his own initiative and proposed that members of the League of Nations cut off their exports of oil to
Italy, which was then engaged in an imperialist assault upon
Ethiopia.

Canada was not as yet an oil-producing state; but the action
of her delegate, in infusing new life into the League of Nations,
might well have led to Mussolini's failure. The Canadian government repudiated his action, and no other state appeared to
seize the initiative. Mackenzie King, just returned to power with
the support of Quebec, was not prepared to affront the opinions
of French-speaking Canadians, most of whom at this time looked
to Italy as the defender of a Latin Catholic civilization.

This unhappy affair, however, is in striking contrast to the
response of Quebec at the time of the Korean War, which, while
not overly enthusiastic, was prepared to support a Canadian contribution to the United Nations police force. So long as international communism remains the enemy, Quebec will be found
in the vanguard of its opponents, and Canadian foreign policy
can be framed in the knowledge that a collective security operation against a Communist aggressor, or any kind of policy
designed to halt Communist expansion, will command French
Canada's support.

The issue of conscription might appear to indicate otherwise.
Canada is the only NATO country not to have introduced compulsory military service, and it is common knowledge that fear
of an adverse reaction in Quebec to such a policy has been largely
responsible for the government's opposition to its introduction.

The issue is of course highly complicated, partly by the fact that there is good ground for disagreement about the necessity of conscription from the standpoint of adequate national defense.

But there is no evidence as yet that conscription is impossible for Canada. Perhaps Quebec's attitude is not so much responsible for this limitation upon the flexibility of Canadian defense policy, and therefore foreign policy, as is the understandable reluctance of leadership to embark upon a daring and difficult experiment. . . .

The British Connection and the Commonwealth

For the last twenty or even thirty years, the Canadian government has been leaning over backwards to avoid the appearance of following Britain's lead. . . .

At the same time, Canada's membership in the Commonwealth is a necessarily conditioning factor, and no statesman responsible for the formulation of our foreign policy can be indifferent to Commonwealth opinion. As Mr. Lester Pearson remarked during the course of the Middle Eastern debate in the emergency session of the House of Commons, "it is in my mind all the time." To this extent Canada's membership in the Commonwealth limits its freedom of action in foreign policy and thus its independence.

But a more significant aspect of the Commonwealth relationship is the fact that it also enlarges and enhances the range and flexibility of Canadian foreign policy. It is by virtue of its membership in the Commonwealth that Canada can and does speak frankly and forcibly to six other nations, in a way which would be impossible if they were not bound together by the Commonwealth tie. On balance, it is probably true to say that any limitation upon a Commonwealth member's freedom of action imposed as a result of its reluctance to offend one or more of the other members is more than compensated for by the greater flexibility in foreign policy which is achieved as the result of having access to the Commonwealth's common stock of information and friendly criticism and advice. . . .

An American Satellite?

An outsider might pardonably suppose that, given the basic fact in Canadian-American relations—which is American power and Canadian weakness—Canada is merely a satellite of the United States. . . .

Perhaps the first point to notice is that there is no necessary connection between cultural penetration or even economic penetration, and political control. It does not follow that because Canadian television audiences see more of Jackie Gleason than of Mr. St. Laurent, they will become more partial to the American way. Quite the reverse may be true. One recalls the old saying about Britain and America, two countries *divided* by a common language. Our very familiarity with the United States may be the cause of our being wary of following its lead on all occasions.

There is similarly no necessary connection between economic influence and political control. The former does not inevitably confer the latter—though it *may* do so, or help to do so. Thus the fact that Americans furnish over 50 per cent of the capital invested in Canadian enterprise does not necessarily mean that they can dictate Canadian foreign policy, or even influence it.

It goes without saying that what the American government will think of what we do is of great importance in determining whether or not we will do it. There is little doubt, for example, that an important reason for Canada's so far refusing to recognize the Peking government is because we know the Americans to be strongly opposed to such recognition. But it is important to put this in proper perspective. It would be foolish to conclude that Washington can veto Canadian foreign policy, as Moscow vetoed the policies of Poland and Czechoslovakia in 1947, when the governments of those two states wished to accept the Marshall Plan aid offered them by America. We could recognize Communist China tomorrow, if we wanted to, and Washington couldn't and wouldn't do much about it.

In so far as the attitude of Washington has been a factor in our policy, it has not been the fear of American reprisal which has deterred us from the course of recognition. It has been, it's argued, the realization that any benefits likely to accrue as a result of such a course—and the British experience suggests that they are not many—would be far outweighed by the fact that Washington would be disillusioned and disappointed, and so less likely to listen as sympathetically to Canadian advice and opinion as has been the case in the past.

Many instances are pointed to of Canadian foreign policy taking a course of which Washington disapproved, or which was disadvantageous to the United States—instances which would be unthinkable if our relations with America were governed by the ordinary considerations of power politics. No satellite could speak to its master as Canada has done on many past occasions—as when Mr. Pearson first narrowly interrogated Mr. Dulles on the meaning of massive retaliation, or, more recently, when Ottawa complained to Washington about its wheat disposal program, or when it announced its intention of proceeding in the face of American objections with an all-Canadian seaway route on the St. Lawrence. The terms on which the United States has built and is operating the radar chains in the Canadian North [see articles on the DEW Line in this section, below] do not suggest that Canadian foreign policy is unduly dependent upon the will of that great neighbor.

In a world dominated by two super-powers, which are themselves dominated by their fear of each other and the prospect of annihilation by nuclear warfare, a middle power such as Canada still has a useful role to play. And among the middle powers, Canada is particularly favorably situated. Her foreign policy may be far from perfect; but there are no reasons beyond her control which prevent its improvement. Though Canada is not a great power, and cannot therefore deflect the course of the great powers by a show of strength, there are many opportunities for a sane statemanship on her part to influence events for the better.

CONTINUITY IN FOREIGN POLICY [4]

When the polls closed on June 10, 1957, the Canadian electorate had prepared for itself a powerful shock. The Liberal

[4] From *Canadian Foreign Policy: Conservative Style*, pamphlet by Robert A. Spencer, assistant professor of history at the University of Toronto. (Behind The Headlines. v 18, no 3) Canadian Institute of International Relations. Toronto. 1958. p 1-14. Reprinted by permission.

party, which had dominated the Canadian political scene for thirty-six years and which had ruled for an unbroken span of twenty-two, went down to defeat. Nine members of a cabinet which a few weeks earlier had seemed unshakable lost their seats. After more than two decades in the political wilderness the Progressive-Conservatives formed a minority government. And nine months later, in Canada's most decisive federal election, the stigma "minority" was erased as they broke the long-lived Liberal stranglehold over Quebec and swept to an unprecedented victory from coast to coast. By nightfall on March 31 Prime Minister John Diefenbaker was assured of a more impressive array of parliamentary support than even the late Mackenzie King had in his heyday.

What were the implications of this revolutionary shift in domestic politics—a shift of even greater magnitude than in the United States in 1952—for Canada's foreign policy? . . .

It is fair to say that only since 1939, possibly only since the end of the Second World War, has Canada had a foreign *policy* which could be enunciated in coherent terms. And . . . the foreign policy of this period was the foreign policy of successive Liberal governments. That is, all the major decisions during the critical two decades when Canada was achieving a more mature international status as an independent state were made by Liberal leaders; and when put together they added up to something that can be called "Liberal foreign policy." . . .

[But] while the policy of the Liberal era was inevitably associated with those who drafted and conducted it, it was a policy which was endorsed by the majority of the Canadian people and by their parliamentary representatives of all parties. The decision, for example, to send a delegation to the charter conference of the United Nations in 1945 was unanimously approved by parliament, and an all-party delegation was sent to the First Assembly. When the North Atlantic Treaty was mooted in 1948, three major party conventions (which by coincidence were meeting that year) passed resolutions in support of the proposal, and parliamentary approval of the Treaty the next year was unanimous. More recently, on so agonizing a question as the admission of Germany to NATO, involving as Senator Croll remarked at the time, a confrontation of a head which must say yes to a heart which must say no, all party leaders supported the government, and only a handful of the CCF stood against it. In all major areas, it seems true to say, the Liberal foreign policy was a bi- or multi-partisan foreign policy. . . .

If one runs down the major problems of high policy which face any western government of the day—atomic disarmament, the unification of Germany, the recognition of Communist China, Arab nationalism in the Middle East, and so on, Conservative policy looks like a continuation of an old line of merchandise under a new label. . . . Where differences . . . [have emerged has been] less in the realm of high policy and more in the more parochial sphere of relations with the United States and with the Commonwealth.

U.S. Guns and Dollars

Relations with the United States is a theme in Canada's foreign relations that is as old as Canada itself. It has also been a recurring subject of debate in the history of Canada's domestic politics, with each of the major parties demanding support at the polls on the grounds that it alone can get more for Canada from Washington, that it alone can stand up to Washington in defense of Canada's interests. It was on the latter point that the Progressive-Conservatives placed their emphasis in the campaign of 1957; and for them it was continental defense and trade that were the critical issues.

The background of Canadian-American differences on defense is essentially a simple one. With the division of the world into two opposing camps after the Second World War, Canadians found that their strategic position had been revolutionized. In the age of atomic bombs, jet aircraft, and guided missiles, the Arctic northland was transformed suddenly into a strategic frontier of immense importance—though less to Canada and more to Canada's neighbor to the south. American military leaders became extremely anxious to place air defenses on the Arctic frontier.

This posed for Canada an extremely critical question. It was only common sense to cooperate in joint continental defense;

but in cooperating with a vastly more powerful and occasionally over-enthusiastic neighbor, how could national sovereignty be preserved? From the time when the basis of joint cooperation was worked out in February, 1947, the Liberal government was at pains to insist that every possible precaution was being taken to preserve national sovereignty. American bases were vetoed (with the exception of Newfoundland, where bases antedated the Act of Union of 1949). All American installations on Canadian soil were under Canadian command. But Liberal ministers were obliged to admit that the problem of control was not easy, when ships, planes, installations and trained personnel to man them, were not available in Canada. And after Korea, with the construction of more elaborate defenses such as radar chains (ruled out as impractical in 1948 but constructed by crash actions since), U.S. defense spending in Canada grew to some $500 million a year, the numbers of U.S. personnel on Canadian soil multiplied, and the threat to Canadian sovereignty correspondingly was magnified. Or so the Progressive-Conservatives argued.

In the light of this stand it was ironical that one of the first steps of Diefenbaker foreign policy should have been to announce (on August 1, 1957) the establishment of NORAD, a joint U.S.-Canadian air defense headquarters at Colorado Springs, with a U.S. officer at its head, a Canadian as his deputy. When the House of Commons assembled in the autumn this issue was hotly debated. There was little disposition on the Liberal benches to quarrel with the need for a joint headquarters. But Opposition members were troubled by the degree of independent initiative to be exercised by the U.S. commander, who was reputed to have received extensive powers of independent decision from President Eisenhower; and the new Secretary of State for External Affairs, [the late] Mr. Sidney Smith, had some awkward moments before the Commons Standing Committee on External Affairs, as he tried to defend an agreement which had been concluded before he assumed office, and about which he appeared to be inadequately briefed.

The essential point of the agreement, which was formalized by an exchange of notes early in 1958, is that far from restricting defense cooperation with the United States, the Conservative government carried it forward another step, and indeed staked out new areas for cooperation in defense production. And, like the Liberal government before it, the new ministry assured Parliament and the country that all necessary precautions were being taken to protect Canadian sovereignty.

Early in September, 1957, three months after his initial victory at the polls, on his first visit to the United States as prime minister, Mr. Diefenbaker took the opportunity in an address at Dartmouth [College] . . . to stress the need for the United States to remove the cause of disagreement, especially in trade and economic matters, "which unresolved may diminish the spirit of understanding which is characteristic of our relationship." Some of these differences arose from the U.S. give-away programs of surplus agricultural products, which profoundly disturbed world markets; others from quotas, bans and other customs devices which hindered the southward flow of Canadian goods. And above all there hovered the threat that U.S. capital was securing a control over segments of Canadian industry so great as to threaten Canada's economic and perhaps even political autonomy.

An October meeting of the Canada-United States Cabinet Trade Committee (a device invented by the Liberals) produced soothing words but nothing concrete. In fact the use by the U.S. Secretary of Commerce of the words "We fixed 'em" not unnaturally stirred up a good deal of resentment. A little later fuel was added to the fire when it was revealed that the ban on trading by U.S. corporations with Communist China also extended to their Canadian subsidiaries; and when U.S. oil imports from western Canada were cut back sharply, U.S.-Canadian relations reached a new low.

It was in these circumstances that President Eisenhower came to Ottawa in July, 1958, (for the first time since just after his inauguration in 1953) to throw his own prestige into the scales. In a three-day visit he established a close personal relationship with Prime Minister Diefenbaker, and addressed a rather academic lecture to a joint session of Parliament. The members received pretty cold comfort. They wanted to hear not a justification of American policies but word of a change in some of them. The President and his Secretary of State departed for

Washington, leaving behind pictures of effusive cordiality, but little in the way of concrete measures to alleviate the differences on matters of trade and economics.

It would, of course, be grossly unfair to blame the deterioration in U.S.-Canadian relations on the advent of a Conservative government. There was a rising tide of anti-American feeling in both parties, and it would have come to the surface whichever way the decision went on June 10, 1957. But the significant point is that from the Canadian side there has been no major shift in policy vis-à-vis the United States. No drastic steps to curb U.S. capital inflow, no higher tariffs, no retaliation for U.S. import restrictions. Indeed one tax measure which the Liberal government inaugurated to protect Canadian magazine publishers was dropped by the Conservatives following protests from American publishers. For the most part Conservative economic policy had conformed to the traditional protest and persuade variety. There is indeed not much difference between Mr. Smith's "hard work, frank talk and good will" and Mr. Pearson's warning that the days of easy or automatic relations were over.

Conservatives and the Commonwealth

There is, of course, a reverse side of the coin. Moves by Canada to strengthen ties with the Commonwealth have the corollary of lessening the bonds with the United States. The preelection statements of Conservatives lent support to the view that this would be the general direction of their policies. Before June 10, Prime Minister St. Laurent had arranged to attend a Commonwealth Prime Ministers Conference in London in June, and had invited the Queen to open the new Canadian Parliament in October. It fell to the new Prime Minister to discharge the duties in connection with these events. Two days after forming his cabinet Mr. Diefenbaker flew to London. As the prime minister of the largest "old" dominion and the leader of a party traditionally standing for close imperial ties, it is hardly surprising that he made a favorable impression. In their final communiqué on July 5, it was announced that the prime ministers had accepted Canada's invitation to a meeting of finance ministers

in September. And in public statements at the time Mr. Diefenbaker advocated an early conference to explore trade and capital
investment within the Commonwealth, and expressed the hope
that Canada's dependence on the United States could be lessened
by diverting up to 15 per cent of Canada's purchases to the
United Kingdom. When the finance ministers met at Mont
Tremblant, Canada's proposal for a full scale trade and economic
conference in 1958 was approved. But Mr. Diefenbaker's 15
per cent proposal was countered by a suggestion by Mr. Peter
Thornycroft, the UK Chancellor of the Exchequer, for the grad-
ual establishment of a free trade area between the two countries.
This provoked widespread concern among Canadian manufacturers and labor groups that Canadian markets would be swamped
by lower-priced British goods; and there was concern that the
talk of large-scale diversion of purchases away from the United
States was responsible for the stiffening American attitude towards
Canada's approaches on trade matters. In his Commonwealth
plans Mr. Diefenbaker had run squarely on the reefs of Canadian
—and U.S.—national interest.

A large and well publicized trade mission visited the United
Kingdom in November-December, 1957, and returned convinced
that Canadian purchases in the United Kingdom could be expanded; but at the conference held in Montreal in September,
1958, little was accomplished on trade questions, beyond the
removal by the United Kingdom of some restrictions on dollar
trading purchases, and an undertaking by Canada to bind under
GATT some preferential items which were already bound as to
margin of preference. Indeed, the most important question raised
at the conference—the need for industrial countries not to place
obstacles in the way of the import of manufactures from under-
developed countries—presented great difficulties for the Diefenbaker government. Unemployment and underproduction in Canadian textile mills had already led it to increase tariff protection
in woolens and it is pledged to do the same in cottons; policies
which are hardly calculated to assist a major export of both the
United Kingdom and the underdeveloped members of the Commonwealth.

In other areas, too, it emerged that Canadian and UK interests were by no means identical. . . . For the most part, though the new Conservative Commonwealth policy may have sounded different, it added up to something closely akin to the bad old Liberal policy. The Conservative government boosted the Canadian contribution to the Colombo plan (inaugurated when the Liberals were in office) and welcomed Ghana and Malaya into the new multiracial Commonwealth (to whose foundations Liberals had made essential contributions), and indeed talked about the Commonwealth in distinctly Liberal terms. Was it Mr. Diefenbaker or Mr. St. Laurent who described the Commonwealth as an association that is "inclusive, not exclusive," and which "encourages and fosters the independence and individuality of its member nations?" Was it the former professor of history [Pearson] or the former university president [Smith] who defined it as "a free association of states, of independent governments choosing to remain in a particular and special type of relationship to each other because . . . there are large areas of agreement between the peoples they represent as to values, ideals, principles and long range objectives"? . . .

Focus on the Middle East

The question of Commonwealth trade shows how Canada tends to be pulled one way by the United States, the other by the United Kingdom. Much light was also shed on her relations with her two partners in the North Atlantic triangle by the crisis in the Middle East. Canadian interest in this area is of very recent origin. Unlike her sister dominions, Australia, New Zealand and South Africa, Canada has not been vitally concerned with the Suez route. She played a very minor role here during the war and after the war refused to contribute to British defense of the region. The Palestine dilemma brought Canadian diplomats and some Canadian soldiers into the picture, but hardly the Canadian people. Then came the Israeli attack on Egypt and the Anglo-French intervention. The (Liberal) Canadian government recognized the nature of the pressure and threat on Israel and the United Kingdom from Nasser's Egypt, but it deplored, indeed was shocked by, the return to gunboat diplomacy, and it feared that it might result in a break between the United States and the United Kingdom, a rift in the Commonwealth, and the disruption of NATO. On the other hand it disliked the high moral tone of the United States, which it realized was not blameless in bringing on the crisis, and it disliked the alliance of Russia and the United States against the United Kingdom.

It was in these circumstances that Mr. Pearson put forward his now famous plan for a United Nations force to facilitate the evacuation of foreign troops and pave the way for a political settlement. For the first time in many years the Canadian government found itself challenged on a major foreign policy issue by the official Opposition. Conservatives denounced Canada's opposition to the Anglo-French "police action," and charged that the United Kingdom had been "let down." Gradually the government succeeded in impressing the Conservatives with the strength of its case. The issue was hardly prominent in the electoral campaign, and in his first foreign policy review in the House of Commons the new Secretary of State spoke of satisfaction and pride in UNEF and referred to its undoubted contribution in arresting a movement "that might have resulted in war." Still, there seems little doubt that there remained lurking a feeling that in an imperial crisis Canada had been found wanting.

This is suggested by the Conservative attitude in the opening stages of the new crisis in July, 1958. At first the government seemed disposed to back the intervention of the United States and the United Kingdom in Lebanon and Jordan, and to echo their political line. But within a few hours Canada's policy changed, and soon Ottawa was ahead of, and indeed going far beyond, either Washington or London in pressing for a summit conference, in admitting Russia's interests in the area, and in stressing the need to come to terms with pan-Arabism.

The two crises of 1956 and 1958 differed in that in the former Britain and the United States were at loggerheads, while in the latter they stood together, condemned jointly by much neutral opinion. But both represented a resort to force, both a flouting of the United Nations and the rule of law, though the case for the United States in 1958 was more plausible than was Suez in 1956. And while the reaction of the Conservative government in 1958 was less prominent than that of the Liberals in 1956, its general attitude was similarly constructive. On both occasions the Canadian government tried manfully to look to the ultimate goal of a political settlement. Indeed, observing Canada's action in the summer of 1958 led one observer to answer the question "What would have happened had the Conservatives been in power at the time of Suez" by replying that if they had been in office only a few weeks, they would have backed the United Kingdom with a "ready, aye, ready"; but if they had been in office a few months, and had been fully apprised of the situation, they would have acted in a fashion remarkably similar to the Liberals.

Plus Ça Change . . .

All this suggests that the Conservative look in foreign affairs is not very new. . . . The traditional ties to the United Kingdom, and the geographical relationship to the United States, for example, remain as valid and inescapable influences for Conservatives as for Liberals.

This helps to explain the fact that . . . [notwithstanding] steps to limit Canadian economic dependence on the United States, by increasing trade with the Commonwealth, this trade must always remain a small fraction of Canada's total, and the United States will remain both Canada's most important market and source of imports in view of the proximity of the two countries and the largely interdependent natures of their economies. Indeed, the Gordon Commission has predicted that the percentage of Canada's trade with the United States will rather increase than decrease in the next two decades. Canadians may regard as tactless and even resent Americans taking us for granted, but it is difficult to disagree with U.S. Ambassador Merchant's statement that Canada's purchases of American goods represent the fulfilment of desires by millions of Canadians, and not something rammed down Canadians' throats by manifest-destiny-minded U.S. senators.

In a notable speech five months before the Liberals were swept from office, Mr. Pearson called for a foreign policy which must be "Canadian, based on Canadian considerations, Canadian values and Canadian interests," and suggested that such an independent foreign policy would inevitably be influenced by four factors which could perhaps be modified but which could not be ignored without peril. These were partnership in the Commonwealth, membership in the United Nations and in NATO, and existence as a neighbor of the United States. These are commonsense points. They represent the fixed poles of Canadian policy as it emerged under Liberal leadership. And a study of Conservative pronouncements on foreign policy does nothing to suggest that either Mr. Smith or his dynamic chief are disposed to quarrel with them.

A Static Foreign Policy?

Does this mean a static foreign policy? Far from it. Foreign policy can never stand still, but must always be evolving with changing circumstances. But it does mean that there is a framework within which Canadian foreign policy must be envisaged; that within that framework, however, there is ample room for alternatives, for evolving imaginative policies, remembering always that a middle power has limited room to maneuver in a world dominated by giants; that there is, as Mr. St. Laurent pointed out nearly a dozen years ago, little use in a middle power recommending action which cannot carry with it the support of the bigger powers.

The importance of the Far East in Canadian-U.S. relations merely underscores the truth of an earlier statement by Mr. Pearson that the issues between the two countries were more numerous and more varied than between any other two sovereign states. Some, such as the United States attitude towards Formosa and still more towards the off-shore islands, involve fundamental issues of peace and war; some are the more parochial issues over matters such as fishing rights and waterways, understandable in view of the fact that some forty rivers cross the international boundary. On ultimate objectives, there is broad agreement; all questions at stake are susceptible to patience and skill. But there is ample room for imaginative statesmanship.

FRONTIER OF UNDERSTANDING [5]

A major factor in the smooth flow of relations between Canada and the United States has been the Treaty of 1909 providing for the joint use of boundary waters and the streams that cross that border.

Prior to 1909 there had been treaties limiting the amount of armed force each country could have on the Great Lakes and on Lake Champlain. The Treaty of 1817 limited Canada and the United States to three ships of 100 tons each armed with an eighteen-pound gun.

Later, in 1871, another treaty provided for joint navigational rights. But prior to 1909 there was no arrangement for the use or diversion of boundary waters. The growing demand for hydro-electric power at the turn of the century made manifest the need for some such machinery.

It was apparent that with a boundary between two countries almost four thousand miles in length, with millions of people living side by side under two separate and distinct governmental systems, old fashioned diplomacy was inadequate to resolve disputes and differences that were bound to arise. Together the two countries were owners in common of a vast property of untold value and it was obvious that a conflict of interest could lead to constant controversy.

Between no two countries in the world is there a boundary of such territorial extent as that between the United States and Canada. Nor is there a boundary between any two countries marked by a common property like the water which marks almost one-half the border between Canada and the United States, or that is as valuable or as essential to the industrial welfare of the people of both countries as is the water between the Bay of Fundy and Lake of the Woods in western Ontario.

[5] From article by Raymond Daniell, New York *Times* correspondent in Ottawa. New York *Times*. sec 11. p21. June 29, 1958. Reprinted by permission.

Treaty of 1909

The Treaty of 1909, drafted by the late Secretary of State Elihu Root, and James Bryce, then British Ambassador to Washington, recognized that these waters were the common property of the people of Canada and of the United States, and that the right to use them for sanitary and domestic purposes, for navigation, for power or irrigation, or any other lawful purpose was a right which the citizens of both countries had in common.

Under the terms of the treaty, no diversion or obstruction of boundary waters or international rivers could be made by either Canada or the United States without the consent of the International Joint Commission which the treaty established. Prior to its establishment there was an International Waterways Commission but its function was purely investigative. The Treaty of 1909 was based largely upon its recommendations.

The commission's six members, three from each country, were given powers of final determination. It is not a diplomatic body nor is a vote taken or evidence presented before an impartial chairman. Its function is quasi-judicial and its members are sworn to decide issues on the basis of facts in a spirit of justice uncontaminated by national interest.

The treaty establishing the commission gave Canadians or United States citizens with grievances the right to seek redress in the courts of both countries. So far as grievances along the border were concerned, its effect was to erase the boundary and to pool the resources of the United States and Canadian courts for the benefit of people on both sides of the waterways. In the forty-six years since the commission has been in existence no national of either country has felt it necessary to invoke this right. . . .

[For discussion of border relations involving the St. Lawrence see Section IV, below.]

Generally, border crossing streams have offered knottier problems than the boundary waters. At first power development was the major problem in the east and irrigation in the west. Recently power development has become as important as irrigation.

An example of the sort of problem that arises when rivers cross from one country to another is provided by the Souris River which rises in Saskatchewan, flows into North Dakota and then back into Manitoba. There an agreement was reached which permits North Dakota one half of the flow of the Souris which in turn permits half its allotment to pass into Manitoba.

One of the knottiest problems ever to come before the International Joint Commission is that of the Columbia River power development. This was set off by an offer of the Kaiser Aluminum Company to build a storage dam on the Columbia in British Columbia to insure a regulated flow for a power dam in the United States. The company agreed to pay for the dam and to transmit 20 per cent of the power generated back to British Columbia.

The 20 per cent power return from the 3.5 million kilowatts that could be generated is not enough, in the view of Canadian officials. They are thinking in terms of 50 per cent. The Columbia River Engineering Board under the International Joint Board is making studies now to find some solution.

COOPERATION IS IMPERATIVE [6]

Canada's proximity to the United States has profound but complicated consequences in her life. There is first of all a constant stream of people back and forth across the border in a manner without parallel between any other two states in the modern world. Most Canadian families have relatives or friends in the United States, and are zealous in exchanging visits. Tourists and business men in large numbers ceaselessly come and go. Restless humans cross and recross at the border points, and have done so for generations. There is also a daily flow of cultural influences over the long frontier through newspapers, magazines, radio and television. These perennial influences cannot but affect Canadian attitudes, and yet this common circulation of cultural blood does not destroy in Canada the sense of national identity.

[6] From background paper prepared by Alexander Brady, Canadian scholar, for the Canadian Institute of International Affairs. Mimeographed text supplied by The Institute. 230 Bloor St. West. Toronto, Ontario. Reprinted by permission.

There continues through it all the will for a distinct Canadian nationhood, which is now not weaker but stronger. Hence the government in Ottawa is not disposed to be merely an echo of Washington without a mind of its own. But there are facts which make imperative the closest collaboration between the two states, and such especially are the allied facts of economics and defense.

Crucial is the fact that, since Canada has been later and slower in development, she has today relative to population more unexploited natural resources than her neighbor. The vast growth of industrialism in the United States, quickened by urgent demand and technical change in the Second World War and its after years, leads the republic to a keener interest in Canada's timbers, metals, and more recently, fuels. She views Canada as a rich frontier of virgin resources conveniently close to her factories, a frontier all the more attractive and significant with the diminution of her own natural wealth. In 1939 she took only 2 per cent of Canada's combined production of aluminum, copper, lead and zinc. In 1950 she took 62 per cent. The two neighbors have become interlaced in a trade greater than that between any two countries in the world. In the twenty interwar years (1919-1939) Canada sent to the United States 38 per cent of her exports, and from that country received 65 per cent of her imports. But in the first postwar years (1946-1950), she sent 48 per cent of her exports and received 71 per cent of her imports. In the two years 1952-1953, her exports to the United States rose to 58 per cent of the total. Related to trade is foreign investment, and since 1945 more than two thirds of the capital from abroad has come from the United States. This foreign capital admittedly is only a small portion of the total investment in Canadian industry (Canadians themselves contribute the bulk) but that derived from the republic is significantly concentrated in the developments of oil, iron ore, aluminum, and such manufacturing as paper and allied products. . . .

Canadians have had no real alternative but to trade abundantly with the United States, which since the Second World War has been able and eager to purchase in large quantities the goods which Britain could not buy. Canadians cannot escape from economic necessity. They must export, or their country suffers paralysis. But apart from other influences, economics today is more than ever closely tied to defense and security, and the combined efforts of the two North American countries in defense imply some attempted integration of their economies.

Since the Second World War the remarkable progress in long-range aircraft and the possibility in the future of atomic warfare have presented a case that no nationalist logic can deny for joint provisions in defending the whole continent. Such provisions are now a valuable corollary to the North Atlantic Alliance, and hence of concern to Britain and the entire Commonwealth. Much of Canada's vulnerability dwells in the simple fact that she possesses fifteen million people in a land of 3.6 million square miles. Two fifths of the area is within the Yukon and Northwest Territories, Arctic in climate, unsuitable for agriculture, and repellent to settlement. This northern land contains only some 25,000 inhabitants throughout its whole vast extent, and across the polar ice lies Soviet Russia. The relatively empty northland is one of the direct approaches to the populated centers of North America, and inevitably its defense must become a joint interest of Canada and the United States. Likewise Newfoundland and Labrador constitute another American strategic area where joint action is imperative, not merely in the interest of the two countries but of the whole system of NATO.

The formal joint action for continental security began in 1940 with the Ogdensburg Declaration and the appointment of the Permanent Joint Board on Defense, which during the war drafted basic plans for defending Canada and Alaska, and after the war remained for both governments a source of expert guidance. The present arrangements fit within the framework established in the forties. Certain broad objectives sought in the collaboration were formally announced in Ottawa and Washington on February 12, 1947:

(1) The interchange of selected individuals in order to increase the familiarity of each country's defense personnel with that of the other.

(2) The general cooperation and exchange of observers in exercises and in testing military material.

(3) The encouragement of common designs and standards in arms, equipment, organization, methods of training, and new developments.

(4) The mutual and reciprocal availability of military, naval and air facilities in each country as may be agreed upon in specific instances.

(5) All cooperation to be arranged without impairing the political sovereignty of either country over the normal activities in its territory.

A joint defense of the continent must involve measures in both countries to promote the most extensive economic development, although in this matter admittedly what is possible or desirable in time of war may not be possible or desirable in time of peace. In one significant sector of the economy, defense production, there has been a zealous effort since 1950 to achieve a major degree of cooperation and integration, and here continuous and fruitful consultations occur between representatives of governments and industry on both sides of the frontier. The more general aim of the two countries must be to ensure the maximum expansion within both and the maximum trade between them, for thereby the economic strength of North America for shouldering the burdens of defense will be enlarged. This common aim is recognized in the agreement between the two countries in November, 1953, to establish a Joint United States-Canadian Committee on Trade and Economic Affairs. The committee consists of members with cabinet rank in Washington and Ottawa, and it is the assumption that their periodic meetings will help to resolve economic difficulties that hamper reciprocal trade between the two countries.

THE DEW LINE: RADAR FRONTIER [7]

Along the northernmost rim of our continent man has undertaken to solve a problem he himself has created: how to survive in the world of the H-bomb. Across the vast Arctic, from Alaska

[7] From "The DEW Line: Radar Frontier," by S. G. Kehoe, free-lance writer living in Kingston, Ontario. *America.* 98:276-7. November 30, 1957. Reprinted from *America* (America Press, New York 17, N.Y.)

to Greenland, determined scientists and workmen have built the DEW (Distant Early Warning) Line as our first line of defense. The DEW Line is the most secret, most expensive and, to many minds, the most valuable project in the U. S. defense armory. It is 3,000 miles long and approximately 600 miles inside the Arctic Circle, at latitude 70°. The United States Government, in agreement with Canada, spent $600 million to construct it.

Scientific advance now has broken the white silence of the Arctic with the thrum of airplanes crossing the top of the world. The airplane is the only means of transportation north of where ships can land men or cargoes, and it is truly the work horse of the North. Two-way radio guides the flyer in this great frozen desert, where no trees or distinguishable landmarks make any part of the country familiar.

Building the DEW Line

In building the DEW Line, transportation presented the gravest of a hundred grave problems. The Canadian Navy loaned their powerful HMCS *Labrador,* equipped with icebreaker, to play an important part in making the project possible. It can land cargoes within 500 miles of the Arctic Circle, and equipment is air-lifted in from there. Navigation in the Arctic is hazardous. There is always ice in some degree, an extreme range of tides, sudden gales, icebergs, fog and uncharted reefs. But the project moves on.

As an experiment, Canada and the United States are jointly planning to send merchant ships out to the eastern Arctic via Bellot Strait. The expensive and dangerous Bering Strait route, now used by the United States as a western approach, is to be abandoned in favor of the Mackenzie River route when Canada takes over the operating of the DEW Line. U.S. Coast Guard vessels, equipped for survey work, will approach from the west, and Canada's naval icebreaker from the east, while RCAF planes maintain their usual ice reconnaissance. The Arctic is unapproachable by ship for nine months of the year.

South of the DEW Line two other such lines, the Mid-Canada and the Pinetree, were jointly installed by the United States and

Canada. They are all part of a detection network extending down the east and west coasts and around the Gulf of Mexico. Foreign and unidentified planes coming from any direction thus will be promptly detected. This top-secret project has fenced our Arctic frontier with a new radar sky-watch. If enemy planes ever attack from over our North Polar regions, every minute of advance warning of their coming will be precious. Minutes may mean the difference between a successful defense and a crippled America.

The Unfriendly Arctic

Almost insurmountable barriers had to be conquered by the hardy men who pioneered the project that made this outpost of defense and communication possible. One unchanging feature of the Arctic is the cold. Fifty degrees below zero is not considered unusual by Arctic standards, nor the ten to twelve feet of ice formed in winter as a result of such low temperatures. The monotonous stretches of ice and snow fall into a thousand fantastic shapes of peaks and hollows. These change, and change incessantly, at the will of the whipping storms and shifting gales. Winds blow up to 80 to 100 miles per hour and chill one to the point at which all movement becomes impossible.

In spring, as the great ice fields break loose, the fury of the storms will sweep them up on shore, to crash and raft and freeze again in overlapping hummocks of wild disorder. Snow, as we know it, does not exist in the Arctic. What snow does fall, usually during September and October, is characteristically like sand. Blizzards and blasts of wind pack it down solidly until one cannot sink through it.

In this grim land the hard-packed snow is, ironically, one of the few gifts of nature. The Eskimos use it as building material and have contributed to the DEW project their experience in its use. They cut large blocks to build their igloos and to insulate the camp huts and buildings. The buildings are constructed in half-spherical igloo shape to withstand winds of high velocity that would rip the roofs from flat-topped buildings and cause perpendicular walls to cave in. Men who must live and work in these difficult and dangerous conditions find it necessary to rig a rope to guide them from living quarters to places of work, since it is impossible to see in the high winds.

Eskimo villages dot the DEW Line, and wherever possible Eskimos are employed in the project. They are bright and cooperative, and in spite of language difficulties learn easily. The fact that they can work around machinery without suffering skin burns from chilled metal makes them a very useful part of the economy. . . .

For . . . strangers, life in the Arctic has a lure that offsets its harshness. Fascinating is the experience of living long months of night. Before total darkness sets in, the November sun rises just enough to give one a glimpse of its upper rim; it circles the horizon clockwise, then drops out of sight for the 145 winter days.

By March the sun has reappeared and the days are getting longer. Daylight increases at the rate of eight minutes a day. Soon one cannot go far without sunglasses. The Eskimo has his age-old type of sunglasses, consisting of a thin piece of bone with a slit in it. The Americans use lenses that can be adjusted to the brightness of the sun; one particular lens is almost totally black. Strange as it may seem, a plague of mosquitoes hits the Arctic during the short break-up season.

Many a strange phenomenon enthralls the newcomer. The bright sunshine, reflected from varied masses of snow and ice, creates wonderful realms of delicate tints and rainbow effects. Ice and snow, mirroring low-lying clouds, produce incredible mirages and optical illusions. You can see for miles on clear days, and it is not uncommon to observe what look like upside-down ships, multiple suns, odd-shaped houses, etc. They can be chased all day in the mysterious North.

Another strange phenomenon is the gaining of weight from the stronger pull of gravity. Lost dogs and lost men circle naturally and irresistibly to the right, as though the spinning of the globe were really felt. Snowdrifts point in the direction of the prevailing wind, and in the Arctic it is remarkably constant from the north. This is how the Eskimo gets his bearings as he travels accurately over astonishingly large areas of unmarked territory.

Here, at the top of the world, radio reception is wonderful. Moscow can be picked up twenty-four hours a day, and the American stations come in clearly.

These and many other interesting facts and conditions help to compensate the unappeasable demands the North makes on man's physical endurance. A lot of work is required just to keep alive in this land. Endurance and skill are needed to exist among the hostile elements.

In the face of such almost overwhelming obstacles, we have now, as it were, raised a defensive roof over our heads, which in the event of a sudden attack will give us time to spring into active defense. The DEW Line is truly a miracle of human achievement.

AMERICANS IN CANADA: FLYING THE DEW LINE [8]

Seventy-one tons of humpbacked, pot-bellied airplane operated by "the world's most perfect airline" took off from a mid-Pacific runway and flew north over the ocean. Seventeen hours later, it returned. It had burned twenty-three tons of fuel and carried its twenty-three-man Navy crew more than three thousand non-stop miles on a flight to nowhere and back—but one vital to America in this atomic age.

This airplane and about a hundred like it are part of the sentry system that guards the United States against the possibility of hydrogen-bomb attack by Soviet Russia. Equipped with radar, the planes fly the seaward extensions of the Distant Early Warning line that arches across the Arctic. The Atlantic Wing is in full operation; the Pacific Wing is in the advanced training stage and will be operating soon. Together, they guarantee the United States a five to six hour warning against attack.

The aircraft that makes these runs is the largest operated by the Navy — a specially adapted Lockheed Super-Constellation packed with 14,000 pounds of radar. It is 116 feet long and

[8] From "Riding The Radar Picket Line," by Gardiner B. Jones, Sunday news editor of the Honolulu *Advertiser*. New York *Times Magazine*. p 18+. May 19, 1957. Reprinted by permission.

has a wingspread of 126 feet. From the ground to the top of the radome it stands thirty-two feet. It costs roughly $5.5 million.

Because the airborne radar system makes staggering demands on its human components, as much comfort as possible is built into each plane. The interior is a foam-rubber wonderland in cool, restful gray-blue, a radical departure from the naked ribbing usually encountered inside a military craft. There are ten foam-rubber bunks, foam-rubber seats for the pilot and co-pilot, and foam-rubber chairs for the men who watch the radar screens. Amidships is a stainless-steel galley containing an electric range, a sink and a refrigerator. Soft lights burn behind frosted glass panels in the ceiling. There is even air-conditioning, a refinement that leads crews to complain about a drying-out of the throat and nasal passages. (Nothing ever is just right in the military service.)

These flying radar sets are currently based at Argentia, Newfoundland, in the Atlantic, and at Barbers Point, Oahu, in the Pacific. They are spaced along the picket course so that their radar sweeps form an unbroken line, somewhat like the string of electric lights marching around the border of an animated advertising sign. The airplane radar is supplemented by the radar of file of destroyers stationed on the surface.

Such an operation requires timing of the highest degree in order to avoid gaps in the line. To meet the rigid time schedule, the Navy adopted a maintenance program copied from commercial airline practices.

The planners have anticipated the foreseeable developments that could disrupt the system—crashes, turnbacks and malfunction of gear. They are ready for them as they occur. But basically they depend on the airplanes to be in top mechanical condition, taking off and landing on the tick.

By following the maintenance system used by commercial airlines, the Pacific Wing is able to have 90 per cent of its equipment in service at any given time, compared with about 70 per cent under standard military maintenance systems. The commercial system involves frequent partial overhauls at or near the operating point and takes an airplane out of service for a comparatively brief period. The military system detaches an airplane to a rear area for several months for a 100 per cent overhaul.

"We are running the world's most perfect airline," an operations officer of the Pacific Wing says. "Actually, nothing can be perfect and we know it, but we're going to come as close to it as we can."

The law of probability eases the Navy's task somewhat. It would be coincidence so rare as to be not worth considering for an attacking force to be able to exploit a hole in the barrier. Flying across thousands of miles of ocean from a distant base, such a force would have to arrive at the hole within rigid time limits of its own in order to slip through. And if it did penetrate, there still is a second barrier—a two-hour warning line off both coasts.

Jamming the radar to prevent identification would serve no purpose other than to notify the Continental Air Defense Command that something untoward was up—which is what the barrier is there for, anyway.

So, on the technical level, it is clear that the radar sentry system ranks high on the scale of infallibility.

At this point, the human element comes in, and as usual—excellent though it is—it is the least dependable part of the system. With proper care and replacement, airplanes and electronic devices go on functioning at peak efficiency without murmur. They do not err in judgment, grow weary, suffer eyestrain, headaches, get edgy from being cooped up or just become sick and tired of what they are doing. All these deficiencies can crop up in the Navy's air radar crews.

These crews are made up of three broad classes of Navy men: the seasoned, young-old pilots who got the salt on their wings flying patrol and transport planes during World War II; the best the Navy has in radar and maintenance technicians; and intensively trained 19- and 20-year-olds who are paying off their service obligation to Uncle Sam as radarscope watchers. It is doubtful that any more capable group of fliers and technicians has ever been assembled inside fuselages.

The problem with the crews is that in an atmosphere of routine and tedium they must operate at peak efficiency every moment in the air. As one officer put it, "A bomber crew is comparatively relaxed until about fifteen minutes before target time. Then everyone springs alert. After the bombs are dropped and the plane leaves the target area, everyone relaxes again. It can't work that way on these missions."

The Navy's main assault on fatigue and the morale problem is launched from the galley. The theory is that if a man is fed what he likes and as much as he wants, he will stay content. The electric ranges aboard the airplane permit the crews to prepare hot meals in flight. There is considerable variety in rations so that the individual crewman has a choice of what he wants to eat. Moreover, he can eat when he feels like it, with the result that any given flight is characterized by continuous munching at one end of the airplane or the other.

In actual operations, each crew makes one mission every 2.3 days. In the Pacific Wing this would mean more than two hundred hours in the air every thirty days, compared with roughly seventy to eighty hours for the average commercial crew. It is an exhausting schedule, but not so exhausting as it sounds. For one thing, the crews are brought up gradually to this level of performance by increasingly longer flights. For another, a radar plane crew is in reality two crews, only one of which is operating the airplane and its gear at a given moment. After 150 hours of flying time, the crews are pulled out of operations for a period of rest, recreation and training.

AREAS OF TENSION: AMERICAN VIEWPOINT [9]

There are probably no two sovereign nations in the world that are closer together than Canada and the United States, no two sovereign nations that enjoy a greater identity of interest.

What are the differences then? Here I am going to take my text from a speech that was recently made before the Canadian

[9] From "The Canadian-American Community of Interest in Political and Economic Affairs," remarks by John Nason, president of the Foreign Policy Association. In *Report of the Canada-United States Conference on Mutual Relations, Washington, D.C., February 7-8, 1955.* American Council on Education. Washington, D.C. 1955. p22-8. Reprinted by permission.

Society of New York by Mr. Henry C. Alexander, president of
J. P. Morgan and Company.

There are, he said, four areas of tension between our countries: (1) the tariff problem, (2) commercial rivalry, (3) differences in matters of global policy, and (4) disagreement on how
to deal with subversion. I shall take up each of these very briefly
in their reverse order.

From a United States point of view, does Canada refuse to
view with sufficient alarm the problem of subversives in its
midst? Is it refusing to face the facts of the international Communist conspiracy or it is simply refusing to be bowled over by
a situation which is not so bad as some people south of the
border think it is, in this country as well as in Canada?

I said earlier that I thought the Canadians had handled the
problem of civil rights or individual liberty with somewhat more
integrity or perseverance than we have in this country. I will
simply throw this out as a minor footnote of difference between
us, that we do handle this problem of what constitutes loyalty
in a different way; and for your consideration and possibly for
argument later, I submit that the Canadians handle it better
than we in the United States.

Differences in matters of global policy: I mentioned also that
Canada views the problems in the Far East somewhat differently
from the way we do. Canadians are involved in these problems
through the Colombo Plan and in other ways.

Canada participated in the United Nations action in Korea,
as did other countries. But Canada, so far as I know, does not
feel the same kind of emotional commitment to Chiang Kai-shek
and the Nationalist Government now located on Formosa that
Senator Knowland and some people in this country feel. Canada
has not recognized Communist China, but Canada has declined
to say that it would not under any circumstances or at any time
recognize the People's Republic of China. Canada in this respect
falls somewhere between the position of the United Kingdom
and the position of the United States.

Canada is less interested in Latin America than is the United
States. While there has been a growing recognition of the countries to the south of the United States on the part of Canada,

Canada is not a participant in the same way in which the United States is, in certain aspects of hemisphere defense and hemisphere activities.

Canada has been criticized at times for not providing as much manpower as is desirable, either for NATO or for the United Nations effort in Korea or elsewhere.

In comment on these differences, it is worth noting that in a free world and in a free society countries should have the right to take different points of view; that this is not only desirable, but healthy; that Canada is a nation of fifteen million people in a rapidly expanding economy and is in a less favorable position for providing manpower than other nations of larger population or less rapid expansion; that while there are differences in our points of view toward global policy, they are not major and they are understandable.

So I turn to the two issues of economic difference, the first of which, according to Mr. Alexander, is commercial rivalry. Is this more than healthy competition? I am talking now not about the production of raw materials, but manufacture, in which Canada is now sixth in size in the world. Is there more competition or is it less healthy between Canada and the United States than between different sections of the United States itself?

Certainly this country has thought it worth putting an $8 billion investment in Canada, and there are three thousand American firms that now have branches north of the border. This suggests that the economy and the industry of the two nations have found it possible to work fairly effectively together.

The fourth issue is the tariff problem, and here I must say I think the difference of viewpoint becomes more significant. There are three aspects which are a problem to Canadians. First, there is the administration of our customs procedures—the delay, the red tape, the irritating practical difficulties which Canadians and others have protested time and again. This is a situation which in the last two years has been to some extent ameliorated; and if certain current proposals now before the Congress of the United States are enacted, further improvement will take place.

Second, there is on the part of this country the use of import quotas against Canadian foodstuffs. We have preached a doctrine in this country for some time about the iniquity of import quotas. We have used our influence in international tariff negotiations and meetings to reduce, where possible, the use of this device to restrict trade. It is not our tariff laws, as most of you know, which bring about this anomalous and inconsistent situation between Canada and the United States. It is a consequence of our policy of maintaining a high standard of living for the United States farmer through maintaining guaranteed prices for certain of his foodstuffs, so that into the Agricultural Adjustment Act were written certain provisions which automatically put into effect import restrictions on Canadian wheat, on Canadian dairy products, and on other foodstuffs when the world price and the United States price have certain relations to one another. This is a source of complaint which Canada has made persistently and consistently and in a very vigorous but courteous fashion.

There is, thirdly, the practice of the United States, or the threat of the practice of the United States, to rid ourselves of our own surplus food products by dumping them in the international markets of the world in a way which jerks the rug out from under the international price which Canada and other food-exporting countries hope to get for their products. It is a practice which we would not like if applied against ourselves. It is a practice which we have repeatedly threatened to undertake, though we have sometimes postponed action in the face of opposition. It has been an unsettling factor in the international markets of the world.

In conclusion, it is obvious that our countries have an extraordinary community of interest. Where we differ politically, it is important to bear in mind that Canada is not yet of the same population size as the United States, and that the problems of leadership which have been thrust on the United States give us certain urgencies which do not yet apply to Canada. Where we differ in our economic points of view, I submit that Canada is basically right and the United States is unfortunately wrong.

How do we strengthen this community of interest which is already so strong? I think we should try to keep the issues clear. I hope the United States will throw its weight around a little less. We could reduce the tension of trade barriers. We could bring about greater exchange of information.

While much is known, and my impression is that businessmen in particular understand each other's operations extraordinarily well, still in the political area there is much to be understood. On the part of the general public there needs to be a greater appreciation, both of the identity and of the difference. There needs to be more of the kind of things which the Canadian Institute of International Affairs is doing, and its counterpart in this country, the Foreign Policy Association, is trying to do.

There needs to be more of the work of the joint committee of the two Chambers of Commerce which has labored so effectively in this area.

As Mr. Wade wrote in one of our Foreign Policy Association's Headline Series on Canada, "Uninformed good will is no longer enough in a world in which international understanding is the last best hope of survival for humanity."

AREAS OF TENSION: CANADIAN VIEWPOINT [10]

Let us turn again to the four points which Mr. Nason laid before us in the order in which he took them, the first one dealing with the problem of subversion. I don't think there is really much difference in our ideas that there is a problem or even, perhaps, of its magnitude. There isn't a great difference between the quiet techniques of the investigating side. A lot of quiet people whom we never hear of on both sides of the boundary are doing a very similar sort of job and with a very close relationship with each other.

It is from there on that it is different to some extent. I am sure that perhaps a partial explanation lies in the fact that there is a difference in the system of government. Where we have, as we have in Canada, a Cabinet system, responsibility for a

[10] From "The Canadian-American Community of Interest in Political and Economic Affairs," remarks by George P. de T. Glazebrook, Minister, Canadian Embassy, Washington, D.C., in reply to remarks by John Nason [see preceding article]. In *Report of the Canada-United States Conference on Mutual Relations, Washington, D.C., February 7-8, 1955.* American Council on Education. Washington, D.C. 1955. p32-4. Reprinted by permission.

problem such as subversion rests primarily with the executive branch. If this job is done badly, those responsible can be voted out of power. If it is done well, nobody has to worry. People on either side of the border may think that the actual way of going at it is right or wrong, but I do not think that anybody needs to worry about the common ground of interest there.

Another political point was on global policy and how far it overlaps. I agree that you find less agitation in Canada about Asian issues. I think that is true of a lot of other questions as well. I represent at this table perhaps a rather phlegmatic attitude, irritatingly so. Perhaps we have too much Scottish blood. I don't know what it is, but we are not very good at "emoting," and that may apply to one thing as well as to another.

The fields of military intervention have been very much the same, except perhaps in the present case of Formosa and the Straits. I would not say we have no interest. That would be far from true. But we have a different interest, in fact a very different relationship to it.

Commercial rivalry was the third point. There certainly is a good deal, and I suppose there always will be. It would be rather peculiar if there were not. I suppose if you asked a good many Canadians how best to improve Canadian-United States relationships, they would say, "Let's have Americans buy more Canadian goods."

On tariffs Mr. Nason did a rather overbalanced picture, I think, of the relative policies there, but certainly there have been difficulties arising out of the customs procedures; and he mentioned in this connection the movement toward customs simplification. It would be appealing to Canadians. We have somewhat similar problems of surpluses and have tried there to keep away from dumping abroad, which is certainly a temptation.

Of course, to me and to a lot of others it is a tragedy that none of us can solve the problem of how, without disturbing a lot of other things, to get surpluses into places where there is not enough to eat. And the motive is very understandable. The difficulties sometimes are such that the cure may be worse than the disease.

Finally, we do have, as Mr. Nason pointed out, one difference, not in the sense of a dispute. This is a relationship between a great power in days when the list of great powers cannot even use up five fingers, and what is sometimes called a middle power, at any rate not a great power. . . . There is bound to be a certain sensitivity and a tendency of the smaller power to feel that at times it is under some pressure. I don't think there is much to go on, but it is a starting point which some people inevitably have.

TALK ABOUT ECONOMIC RELATIONS [11]

Q. What would you like to tell Americans, Mr. Prime Minister, about how they might improve their relations with Canada generally?

A. There must be no cleavages in our unity, or unresolved differences. At all costs—as differences which exist from time to time among friends, neighbors, even among close relations, must be resolved—our peoples must act with infinite forbearance in order to assure the removal of existent differences. We understand each other and can and must speak frankly to each other.

Q. What do you say about the fears of some American businessmen that they are going to encounter difficulties in their operations in Canada?

A. There will be no difficulties encountered in any way, and any such fears must be based on what was a major "export" during the election campaign—an unjustified propaganda of fear.

Q. Do you foresee closer ties between Canada and Great Britain and the other countries of the Commonwealth than have prevailed in past years?

A. Canada must have markets. If our trade is restricted anywhere by state action, we have to act elsewhere in order to assure an expansion of our trade. To that end, I advocated the

[11] From an interview with John Diefenbaker, Canadian Prime Minister. *United States News & World Report.* 40:72-6. April 18, 1958. Reprinted from *United States News & World Report,* an independent weekly news magazine on national and international affairs published at Washington, D.C. Copyright 1958 United States News Publishing Corporation.

convening of a Commonwealth Trade and Economic Conference at the Commonwealth Prime Ministers [meeting] in London during July, and it will convene in Montreal in September next.

Q. Do you think Canada actually will divert 15 per cent of its trade from the United States to Britain?

A. At no time did we say that we were going to divert 15 per cent. I said, as an example, that, if 15 per cent were diverted, the result would be to bring about a reasonable deficit in our trade with the United States and, at the same time, assure us markets that are virtually nonexistent today.

Q. Where would the sterling countries get the dollars to buy from Canada?

A. That's one of the problems which will be faced by this conference. History shows that where there is a will there is a way, and I think that is the spirit which will actuate the representatives at this conference.

Q. Do you feel that Canada's trade with Communist China should be expanded?

A. I see no reason why there should not be a pronounced extension of our trade with China, but strictly excluding strategic materials.

Q. Mainly in agricultural products?

A. There is a wide field even within the limits of strict exclusion of strategic materials.

Q. Does your Government favor a possible recognition of the regime in Peiping?

A. We have never given any indication of that. That matter is subject to review, but recognition is in no way necessary as a basis for trading relations. . . .

Q. Is the recession still a serious problem in Canada?

A. While Canada's present economic difficulties began before they became apparent in the U.S.A., we're naturally being affected today by the economic dislocation in the United States. However, I feel sure that we are well on the way back to full recovery.

Q. In the future development of Canada, do you foresee a weakening of the ties with the United States?

A. No; none whatever. We welcome American capital. We have only to think for a moment how terrible our position would be in Canada if the U.S.S.R. were in the same relative position to us as is the United States of America. That, to me, is the simple answer to those who say that the attitude of the Progressive-Conservative Party is anti-American. It is far from it. It is pro-Canadian.

Q. What does this mean in terms of American investments in Canada?

A. We ask—when capital comes into Canada, when development takes place here under the aegis of American corporations —that development shall be for the primary benefit of Canada. And I'll give you an example of the kind of thing that has caused irritation. Some American corporations won't permit Canadians to buy equity stock in the Canadian subsidiary. The parent company comes into Canada and establishes a subsidiary. Then, at the end of the year, it sends its profits—with the deduction of 15 per cent of corporation tax on profits sent outside Canada—to the United States. Then the Canadian investors have their share come back from the United States less 15 per cent.

Q. You mean Canadian owners of stock in American companies?

A. Yes. Secondly—once more clearly re-emphasized in the recent action of preventing the sale of cars to China by a Canadian subsidiary—we believe that the direction of business in Canada must be determined on the basis of Canadian interest, and not on the basis of the interest of any other country. When my friends from the United States question our stand in this regard, I simply ask, what would their attitude be should Canadian companies establishing in the United States follow similar courses of action?

Q. Nevertheless, do you see a major role for American capital in Canada's future?

A. Absolutely! There's to be no discouragement whatsoever. In fact, every encouragement to that end will be given—subject always to the necessity of investment being for Canada's benefit.

Q. Do you plan legislative action to deal with the problem?

A. I simply point out the problem as I did in a speech I delivered at Dartmouth College in September, and said then:

> Canada can compete for her share of the market of the world, providing other nations follow recognized competitive practices. The share of the world market for wheat by the United States has been increasing in

recent years by its policies of surplus disposal, and that increase has come about mainly at the expense of Canada's export trade, which has been decreasing. The surplus-disposal legislation of the United States has made it difficult, if not impossible, for Canada to maintain its fair share of the world's market. Canada cannot compete for agricultural markets against the dominant economic power of the United States, with its export subsidies, barter and 'tied-to' deals and sales for foreign currency.

I have never, indirectly or at all, suggested legislative action. I have pointed out the problems and have asked for cooperation in their solution.

Q. Will your Government urge American companies toward that end?

A. Well, naturally, I expect them to realize our feelings in that regard—a perfectly legitimate expression of a pro-Canadian viewpoint—and, I reiterate, not one in any way anti-American. But I do want to see Canada's development insured for Canadian purposes and ends. And we want company policies determined— within reason—in Canada.

Q. You think the Americans themselves should do something about these "irritations" connected with U. S. capital in Canada?

A. Oh, I do, and that has been made very clear as the Canadian viewpoint, without regard to political party, in the Gordon Report—the report of the Royal Commission to investigate Canada's economic future. That report was made under the chairmanship of Mr. Walter Gordon, who was one of Mr. Pearson's [Lester B. Pearson, leader of the Liberal party] chief lieutenants in the recent election.

Q. What about the complaints that the American Government is underselling Canada in wheat and other things?

A. We are partners in the North Atlantic Treaty Organization and in the maintenance of freedom through that instrument. It doesn't make sense to me that any one of the partners should so act as to detrimentally weaken the economic strength of another partner.

The United States has assumed vast international responsibilities. The United States has been generous, beyond words to describe, in its outpouring of treasure to assure that the shield of freedom will be preserved. But in the economic field we have taken strong objection—and when I say we, I mean Canadians as a whole—to policies that are in derogation of our joint responsibility under NATO. As an instance, I might mention the "fire sales" of agricultural products to various countries.

Q. Fire sales?

A. Fire sales. Selling at ridiculously low prices *when*—and I underline that word "when"—coupled with a demand that the recipient country shall for a designated number of years purchase from the United States x quantities of agricultural products in the future.

We've no objection to fair competition, but a competition which has in it the gobbling up of markets for the future in that manner is in our opinion in derogation to GATT [General Agreement on Tariffs and Trade] and to our responsibilities to each other under the NATO concept.

There's been some improvement recently in this regard, and every improvement is regarded as beneficial, but there's still more to be done in that direction. I want to re-emphasize what I said: It isn't the competition for today's markets that we take objection to, but it's adding as a condition, precedent to the acceptance of today's bounty, that the recipient nation shall assure a designated share of its market in the future.

Q. Hasn't the United States done this in order to get rid of its own agricultural surpluses?

A. That's perfectly true, but it does not afford an excuse. What I object to is the adding on of the kind of proviso that, in return for the bounty of today's market, the recipient country has to guarantee designated quantities of its future markets.

Q. What does that do to the Canadian wheat market?

A. It undermines a major element in our export trade.

Q. There has been some talk of a U. S. import quota on lead and zinc. What would be your attitude on that?

A. The imposition of an embargo on zinc and lead will have detrimental effects—not only on the Canadian producers of these products, but in general—for we believe unilateral action of this kind is not conducive to our trade relations in general. Canada is a major customer of the U.S.A., and such action cannot but have adverse effects.

Please do not lose sight of the fact that Canada is numbered among the great trading countries of the world. While desirous of doing business with all nations, our trading world has become increasingly confined to the United States, which takes 60 per cent of our exports and provides 73 per cent of our imports.

Even in agricultural products, Canada buys a larger volume of American agricultural products, by some $100 million, than Canada sells to the United States.

United States exports to Canada are almost as much as the total sales it makes to all Latin-American countries. Canada is the United States' greatest customer and the United States is Canada's greatest customer. What you are buying from us is largely raw materials or semi- or partially-manufactured materials, for the United States tariff system prohibits any major import of manufactured goods.

This concentration of trade in one channel contains inherent dangers for Canada. It makes the Canadian economy altogether too vulnerable to sudden changes in trading policy at Washington. Canadians do not wish to have their economic, any more than their political, affairs determined outside Canada.

Canada has always purchased more from the United States than the United States has purchased from Canada. This imbalance is now running to record proportions. In our commodity trade in 1956, Canada purchased from the United States goods to a value of $1,298,000,000 more than the United States purchased from Canada.

Q. On these points of friction in economic matters—

A. I'm not going to adopt your word "friction." Rather, they are points of disagreement. Everything should be done to resolve them in a spirit of friendship and good will. We have parallel interests. We need you for our survival and you need us. We are cooperating in defense, but cooperation economically is equally necessary.

Q. Do Canadians generally feel that the United States has not cooperated sufficiently in the economic field?

A. I would say, in the economic field, that Canadians generally feel that there has not been that degree of cooperation which is necessary to assure that unity which is of the essence in our struggle for survival against the forces of communism. We share each other's viewpoint in the fundamental things of life. We cooperate without fear and in full understanding in defense. Why not a similar spirit in our economic affairs?

Q. Is that feeling directed at the American Government mainly, or at the American business community?

A. That, of course, you will have to answer yourself. That's an answer that I can't give. However, the marketing policy of agricultural products is state directed and controlled.

Q. Do you have any clear idea of how great Canada's potential resources are? Have they been measured?

A. As yet there has never been a complete assessment as to the potential total of those resources. And that's one of the things that we expect to undertake. You had a summary of American resources in the Paley report [made by the President's materials policy commission in 1952], which indicated that, in not too many years, by 1975, the United States would be in large measure a "have not" country in those things that are needed today for technological advancement. We're a "have" country in resources.

Q. Where do you think the capital will come from to develop the north country?

A. We shall continue to warmly welcome foreign capital, and we hope that Canadians will invest to a greater extent than heretofore in their own future.

Canadians have been very conservative in their investment in, and in the development of, their own country, but are now beginning to develop a more general interest in participating in investment in their country's future.

Q. What kind of development do you foresee?

A. Until the last decade few had any realization of the vast hidden resources of these northern areas extending to the islands in the Arctic Circle. Those islands, capped with ice, are now revealed to be the repositories of tremendous mineral resources.

Q. Iron ore, copper, or what?

A. All of the basic metals. Then there's the Mackenzie River area: The oil potentialities there are greater than other generally recognized oil-potential areas. We intend, in those areas for which the Dominion Government is responsible, to provide access roads to resources; also, to see to it that rail transportation, where feasible, will be readily available. And—going back a moment to an earlier question, the question of investment—may I point out this: The American investor today is in a more advantageous position in making development investment in Canada than is the Canadian. In connection with oil and mineral exploration, the tax write-offs in the United States are more favorable and more realistic than ours, with the result that Canadians—because of our laws—do not enjoy equality with Americans in investment in Canada. Consideration will be given to making the necessary tax changes in order to equalize opportunities for Canadians.

Q. In such things as depletion allowances?

A. Yes, the depletion allowance should be more favorable.

Q. In this development of the North, can you get large numbers of people to live up there where it's so cold?

A. That question could be asked just as well of the people who are residing in similarly located areas of Norway and the U.S.S.R., where vast developments have taken place.

Settlement has brought about a very material change in climatic conditions. Whether settlement would achieve that in these northern settlements or not, it has been shown that within the Arctic regions it's quite possible to have extensive population and development, and that climatic conditions do not operate as a serious deterrent.

Q. In the development of these minerals and resources, do you think that more of them should be processed within Canada than in the United States?

A. Yes, I certainly do. We want, to a greater extent than heretofore, to have the processing within Canada of our resources. We realize that there will always be a large amount of export in raw-material form or semiprocessed materials, but the percentage today is so high as to constitute a serious detriment to our national well-being.

Q. Would this include the iron-ore industry as well?

A. It would include all resources. I should point out that resources within the provinces are within the exclusive legislative jurisdiction of the provincial governments, and that any policy that we might have would be subject to these constitutional limitations.

AGAINST ANTI-AMERICANISM [12]

Dr. Hilda Neatby's criticism of Canadian education, reports of the extent of American capital investment in Canada, the construction of the DEW Line, the resignation of Mr. Frank A. Tinker, United States vice-consul at Toronto, the suicide of the late Mr. Herbert Norman, the debate on the Trans-Canada Pipe Line bill, the current Canadian wheat surplus, and dozens of other apparently unrelated matters of the last few years have at least one thing in common: Each has been the occasion for a spate of articles, addresses, and editorials dealing with relations between Canada and the United States. In turn, the bulk and the nature of this comment have occasioned, from time to time, further comment on "the current wave of anti-Americanism" in Canada. The most casual acquaintance with North American history should settle the fact that this note of concern is not new. . . .

There is little reason to believe that this general concern over national identities and national influences will not continue, and no reason why it should not. Never before, perhaps, have intelligent Canadians been under a sterner and more urgent obligation to scrutinize the values they profess to hold and to make unflinching judgments according to those values. And never, perhaps, have they had a greater obligation to examine critically their relationship to the United States of America in all its aspects—military, economic, diplomatic, cultural, and so on. Each adjective suggests a new crisis demanding judgment. But in each of these areas, judgment is likely to be clouded, even perverted, by our unawareness of a moral and semantic failing—our habitual use of the epithet "American" . . . as a term of outright abuse. . . .

[12] From "An Offense Unto Charity: Personal Reflections on a National Attitude," article by Walter E. Swayze, professor at Queen's College, Kingston, Ontario. *Queen's Quarterly.* 64, no3:326-37. Autumn 1957. Reprinted by permission.

In terms of physical appearance and of intellectual, moral, religious, and social climate I have found greater differences between neighborhoods a couple of miles apart in Winnipeg than I have found between either of these neighborhoods and corresponding neighborhoods in American cities two thousand miles from Winnipeg and several hundred miles from each other. Suburbia is Suburbia on either side of the border. Yet to many of us Canadians, life south of the unguarded frontier (which incidentally, is jealously, zealously, but somewhat capriciously defended by the thinnest of thin skins) is perfectly homogeneous and quite unlike anything to the north of it. . . .

In over seven years of living in the United States and several subsequent visits I have had hundreds of experiences of Americans hypostatizing a Canadian stereotype ridiculously at variance with the multiplicity and variety of my own experiences of Canada, but rarely has this stereotype been unflattering, never hostile or malicious. Yet many of us Canadians rarely use the word "American" except in terms of a stereotype that is viciously untrue even to our own experience of what constitutes American. Those of us who consider ourselves the intelligentsia are frequently the worst offenders. The average citizen is likely to be quite happy with his American automobile, American movies, American vacations, and American attitudes, until an anti-American headline jars his composure for a day or two. From time to time intelligent discussions of Canadian attitudes to the United States do appear. . . . On the whole, however, the tone of discussion of American institutions and culture in Canadian faculty common rooms and clubs, and in private homes of Canadian academicians and other professional men is so violently, irrationally anti-American that an accurate transcript of the conversation would not be acceptable dialogue in a third-rate problem novel. . . .

Actual examples are likely to be so bizarre as to seem pointless, but one must begin somewhere. Years ago when I was doing graduate work at Yale, my wife and I received a letter from an academic friend who knew something of Canada and of England, but nothing of the United States. After the usual anti-American tirade, he expressed the hope that we would soon be able to leave that Sahara of mad materialism and return to a place that had some "real culture." The question of definition may be important. However, there we had daily access to a library many times the size of the largest Canadian library; a faculty whose annual list of scholarly publications might compare favorably in quantity and quality with the entire output of all Canadian colleges and universities, and yet a faculty which enjoyed a most stimulating personal relationship with their students. . . .

Yale, of course, cannot be used to represent any American average, but it does represent one large and significant area of American culture. Some American colleges and universities are travesties of any reputable concept of higher education, and there are enough mediocre institutions to depress the most optimistic educator. But few Canadians are aware of the hundreds of good American institutions that quietly and unassumingly do well the work they have been doing, for generations, in some cases, without their names ever reaching Canadian headlines. . . .

Certainly there are cultural Saharas and educational Limbos south of the border, but we Canadians know that they exist chiefly through the vehement and determined protests of articulate, informed Americans who want to do something drastic about them. The wholesale indictments of American education that we Canadians indulge in from time to time are usually uninformed or unconsidered. . . .

The same oversimplification of judgment applies in other areas. Take McCarthyism for example. No one can deny the continuing presence—and the menace—in the United States of the mind and temperament that produced McCarthyism, but no one has denounced it and resisted it more courageously, articulately, and confidently than Americans themselves. The tradition of individual freedom and individual responsibility is no minor tradition, but the dominant one. At the height of the late Senator McCarthy's influence and power, two distinguished professors at Harvard conducted a country-wide solicitation for funds for the express purpose of defeating Senator McCarthy and his colleagues. The roster of universities and other organizations that resisted all attempts to limit freedom of thought and expression by arbitrary means is far more impressive than the list of those that capitulated. The American Association of University Professors, which investigates all reported cases of infringement of academic freedom and tenure and censures the administrations of institutions in which "unsatisfactory conditions of academic freedom have been found to prevail", and is not afraid to blacklist such giants as the University of California, Ohio State, and Rutgers, for example, nor too proud to investigate complaints in the most obscure little colleges imaginable, had nine institutions on its censured list as of April, 1957, and had members in over a thousand "approved institutions" in continental United States. . . .

Race relations in the American South are the subject of much heated discussion in Canadian common rooms, living rooms, newspapers, and journals. Having lived in the South for four years, I have experienced the humiliating and inhuman absurdities of segregation, including a fifteen-foot palisade down the center of a drive-in theater, the polite, worried refusal by a colored caretaker to wash his hands in my bathroom which he had just repaired, and the sending of all colored help, male and female, from all over a college campus, to segregated washroom facilities adjoining the dressing room of a gymnasium for white southern ladies. But I know that almost everyone involved in these situations, regardless of color, considered them outmoded absurdities. I have read several hundred "themes" or essays written by white southern students on various aspects of the racial question, and with the most determined effort of memory I can recall only one that was anti-Negro, anti-integration. When the first colored graduate student was admitted under a Supreme Court ruling that forced the college to admit him if equal colored facilities were not available for him elsewhere in the state, he was welcomed by students and faculty alike. When a local chapter of the AAUP discussed the feasibility of regional meetings with delegates from neighboring colored institutions, the only objection raised came from a venerable white-haired, devout Methodist from northern Ohio. . . .

I am not denying the strength of violent racial hatreds in the South, the complexity of the problems involved in integration, nor the disquieting trend of legislative reaction on state and Federal levels to recent decisions of the Supreme Court. But I do know that millions of Americans in the South as well as in the North are working quietly, tirelessly, even heroically, toward the reduction of these hatreds and the solution of these problems, and few of these people appreciate the gratuitous, self-righteous moralizing and advice that characterize the editorial utterances of the Canadian intelligentsia, undergraduate and graduate. A more persistent concern with our own attitudes to our Indians and our Eskimos might do more good on both sides of the border. . . .

Few of us Canadians know the American scene at all well, and far too many of us, whether we know what we are talking about or not, fall into the habit of using the world "American" to denote only the worst aspects of our subject. The result is often a complete lack of logic and of good manners. Canadians who have done years of graduate work and even post-doctoral study in American universities and libraries, supported by American fellowships and grants-in-aid of research (or Canadian fellowships and grants provided partially or even largely by American foundations), whose articles have been published in American journals and whose books have been published by American presses, who have relied on American learned societies for much of their professional association, who have dozens of outstanding works of American scholarship on their recommended reading lists for every course they teach, and who are proud to have their best students accepted by American graduate schools, may still find themselves talking in derisive terms of American education and American scholarship, as if nothing on earth were more ridiculous. One good friend recently said in impatience, "This is the third American text that I've received in the last few weeks that is very badly written. Listen to this!" Perhaps these American texts were badly written. But the same friend had been most enthusiastic about several other American works that we had discussed in recent months, and he never used the abusive epithet "American" in connection with any of them.

What is true of scholarship is true of almost everything else. Good movies are never connected with Hollywood.

Mediocre or bad ones always are. Elvis Presley and Bill Haley are American, even though English teenagers "dig" them more violently than their American counterparts, but the New York Philharmonic-Symphony is just a good orchestra, as are a dozen or so others. The Berkshire Music Festival and similar festivals of music and dance are rarely called "American"— by many Canadians. (In the interests of fair dealing and good relations the Canadian Government Travel Bureau has found it wise to point out repeatedly to American visitors that the word "imported" on price cards and in advertisements usually means "Made in the United States of America.")

"American" is often applied to things that are strange and therefore suspect, but which are not really or necessarily American at all. Spellings, pronunciations, idioms, grammatical conventions listed in the strictly British *Oxford English Dictionary* are frequently condemned as "American" by vigorous but poorly informed purists who have been brought up on or have grown accustomed to American preferences without being aware of the fact. What is true of language is true of other matters. Many of these are insignificant in themselves, and it may seem petty even to mention them, but they are all related to an important issue. . . An offense unto charity is not without consequences. Presumably the man who fell among thieves was eventually better off than the priest and the Levite who passed by on the other side. The United States is a hardy nation and will not suffer any decline and fall because of anti-American feeling in Canada. But Canadians will suffer, and not because we make an American vice-consul feel that he is unwanted and that his nation is slighted, or because other Americans are offended. Canadians will suffer whenever we use anti-Americanism as a cloak for our own ignorance, whenever we use American institutions and policies as a scapegoat for our own sins of omission, whenever we blame American inventiveness and energy for what is really our own lack of vision. Again and again contempt for an articulate American patriotism goes hand in hand with a complete lack of faith in Canada.

This is no plea for blind and abject capitulation to American influences, for acceptance of all American values. It is a plea for us to get to know what we are really talking about whenever we use the epithet "American," to get to know facts as well as we can before we try to pass judgment on them. Once we really understand a certain situation, the more critical we are, the better. Then, perhaps, we can break the all-too prevalent habit of loudly condemning a certain aspect of American life and then hailing the same thing as progressive Canadianism a few months or a few years later. As the Canadian economy expands, as Canadian national consciousness gains greater self-awareness and articulateness, as Canadian influence in international affairs becomes greater, the constant revaluation of all aspects of our relationship with the United States becomes more and more imperative. Continual self-righteousness, superior boorishness will rob us of the friendship, guidance, and support of some of our warmest, best, and most valuable friends and keep us from understanding our own strengths and weaknesses. Uncritical yielding to American pressure is bound to be dangerous, whether the pressures be good or bad in themselves, and similarly, an uncritical or hypercritical hostility to everything that is or is considered to be American can be equally dangerous. It may be human nature to despise or resent Americans for being efficient, successful, powerful, or impressive; it may be human nature to feel superior every time we read or hear of corruption, ignorance, cruelty, or stupidity south of the border, regardless of corresponding deficiencies in our own backyard; but it is not usually very helpful.

We must try to form and retain some picture of the incredible variety, the unexpected paradoxes and blatant contradictions of American life and culture. In doing so, we must remember that like the citizens of all other mature, free nations, Americans have a gift for self-criticism of the most penetrating sort, a genius for washing their own dirty linen in public. We must be prepared to acknowledge and praise virtues, whether they be American or not, because they are virtues, and condemn vices in the same way and for similar reasons. And before making judgments, we must remember the mote and the beam and remind ourselves that censure abroad rarely remedies failings at home. By admitting the excellence of eminent Americans and

American organizations and institutions, we shall not be belittling the stature and the achievements of eminent Canadians and Canadian institutions. Rather, we shall heighten the value of our praise by proving that we can judge according to standards that remain standards in spite of the emotional boundaries of nation, race, and creed.

As we mature as a nation we must, as we are doing in an ever-increasing number of important fields, firmly insist on taking over responsibility for things that the United States has done well for us and is still doing well, simply because we cannot achieve and maintain our own individuality as a nation if we do not do such things. If we have to make demands or protests, they will be more effective if they are not accompanied by hysterical finger-pointing and self-righteous smugness.

Right now, whether we like the situation or not, some of the strongest influences on Canadian life and thought are American. There is no doubt about that. But there is no doubt that a careful scrutiny and evaluation of those influences and of comparable areas of our own life and thought will help us make the greatest steps toward our own maturity as a nation.

IV. ECONOMIC GROWING PAINS

EDITOR'S INTRODUCTION

In the boom year of 1957 Canada was described as the most rapidly developing country in the world. Since the economic recession of 1958 writers have been more cautious. Forecasts on the economic future, still optimistic, are nevertheless less superlative in tone and more measured in their prognostications. The articles in this section are meant to provide a rapid look at the potentialities of this "young giant in infancy" and at the growing pains it is experiencing in its economic development.

The first three articles provide a general look at the present development and future potential. First, a correspondent for the British *Economist* notes the "contagious confidence in Canada's own future" but cautions that: (a) the need for capital to develop natural resources has led to foreign control over important sectors of the economy; (b) Canada's economic well-being has become perhaps unhealthfully tied to the prosperity of the United States. The second article describes the optimism which infected Canada in 1957 when its largely undeveloped resources were "being tapped at breakneck speed." The third selection provides an over-all look at the natural resources and economic potential of the country and concludes that economic strides should continue to be vigorous.

The three articles which follow concern the economic significance of the long-awaited opening of the St. Lawrence Seaway. It means, the writers tell us: electric power for industries and for commercial and residential use; the extension of shipping to inland Canadian ports; help in the exploitation of iron ore in Labrador; a boon to tourism; and an uprooting of communities.

Half of Canada is Arctic land and thus much of Canada's potential is tied to the Arctic potential. This is the subject of the next selection, in which Walter Sullivan of the New York *Times* vividly describes the Arctic—what it is, its natural resources, its people, and how it is being exploited and changed.

Another selection points to a gloomy side of Canadian development; the writer finds that if Canadians do not take precautions the new industrial development will exaggerate the contrast between rich and poor. In the final article United States Senator Neuberger of Oregon describes one program aimed at minimizing such contrast: the monthly allowances paid to all families with children.

GROWING PAINS OF A YOUNG GIANT [1]

One's first impression when the plane loses height over Newfoundland is of an unfinished struggle. The Atlantic is reluctant to relinquish its sway, undisputed for so many hundreds of miles, and the countless lakes seem locked in a struggle for supremacy with the land. This feeling of the unfinished grows stronger as the journey proceeds across this continent so vast that the sixteen million inhabitants concentrated in a relatively thin strip north of the United States border still seem like pioneers on a bridgehead. The skeletons of new skyscrapers in booming Toronto or Vancouver, the mushroom oil towns in the west, the scarcely tapped resources of the north, all strengthen the impression that this is no mere boom, but part and pattern of an industrial revolution.

The other immediate impression, for an innocent straight from Europe, is of the American-ness of the country. It is not so much the accent which is striking. The little Hillmans, overwhelmed amid the giant North American cars, seem symbols more eloquent than the statistics about foreign investment in Canada (American investments account for over three quarters of the total, British for only 17 per cent). But this impression becomes blurred. Every third Canadian is of French origin, and for him "Americanism" is a thin veneer superimposed on an outmoded French parochial background. In Ottawa the Houses of Parliament, modeled closely on Westminster, embody nos-

[1] From "Bird's Eye View of Canada: Growing Pains of a Young Giant." *Economist.* 184:981-2. December 15, 1956. Reprinted by permission.

talgia for the Old Country. In Vancouver, Calgary and many other places a Scots accent is the best possible passport. Every reference to United States influence—even a Freudian verbal substitution of president for prime minister, or state for province —is greeted resentfully; and Canadians' comments on their overshadowing neighbor contain an element of derisive envy.

The trend towards closer integration with the United States is undeniable. Canada has become the fourth trading nation of the world, with a turnover scarcely lower than that of Germany; but three fifths of its exports go to the United States and three quarters of its imports come from the same source. Its postwar surplus on current payments has turned into a deficit, balanced (and partly prompted) by an inflow of foreign, chiefly American, capital. By the end of last year its gross liabilities to other countries had reached $14.7 million, double the postwar level, but even more striking has been the steady increase in direct foreign investment in Canadian industry. It may be argued that the deficit is a small proportion of the total turnover and the foreign contribution a small share of domestic investment. Nevertheless it has led to foreign control over important sectors of the economy. Whether because of caution on the part of Canadian investors or because the American giants can spread their risks more easily, it is American capital that has paved the way in oil and postwar mining, thence spreading to manufacturing. As early as 1953 well over one third of manufacturing and more than half the oil and mining development in Canada was in American hands. Today, two thirds of the large enterprises in these fields are controlled by foreign, predominantly American, capital.

The reactions vary. Mr. Manning, the prime minister of Alberta, welcomes the influx of American oil capital into that province. It has brought such prosperity that the Albertans are said no longer to label dates as BC or AD, but speak of BL and AL, in reference to the striking of oil at Leduc, near Edmonton, in 1947. Mr. Manning, who has been enabled to reduce the provincial debt while expanding social services, is content with nominal ownership of the oil and control over its rate of production. But the sophisticated young intellectuals of Ottawa are more perturbed. They argue that the situation will not redress itself automatically through the growth of the country's economy. They point out that many of the companies concerned are beyond the reach of the Canadian investor: some are expanding on ploughed back profits; others are subsidiaries, whose shares are not quoted on the Canadian market and whose parent companies are too big for the Canadians to buy a controlling interest. They complain that tax reliefs offered to American-controlled companies under a double taxation agreement now being revised provide no inducement to bring Canadians into partnership. Some of them also argue that the inflow of American capital may neutralize the traditional fiscal weapons against inflation.

The clash of ideas on this subject took vivid shape in June [1956], when a debate over a pipeline to be built by an American company led to one of the biggest rows in Canadian parliamentary history. Yet, with varying degrees of enthusiasm or reductance, the trend is generally accepted. The chief argument in its favor is that without this support Canada would not have been able to carry out its industrial revolution while shouldering a heavy defense burden and ensuring a rising standard of life to a fast growing population. The minority of pessimists who complain that "when the United States sneezes, Canada catches flu" are told that this risk is shared with the whole western world and is anyway much exaggerated. Indeed, much of Canada's economic activity seems based on the assumption that the United States has found a vaccine against depression. This faith is coupled with a contagious confidence in Canada's own future. Even a swift flight across this land almost the size of Europe is enough to bring it home that one has had a glimpse of a giant in infancy. It is to the north and to the future that the Canadians look to restore the economic balance of the new world.

BOOM ACROSS THE BORDER (1957)[2]

Some of the most exciting events of all are taking place just across our northern frontier. Our Canadian neighbor is the most rapidly developing country in the world today.

[2] From "Canada: Giant on our Doorstep," news story. *Senior Scholastic.* 70: 11-14. May 10, 1957. Reprinted by permission.

Canadian industries are mushrooming in faraway areas that only a few short years ago were wilderness. Canada's fabulous —and largely undeveloped—treasure house of natural resources is being tapped at breakneck speed.

Output of minerals (including copper, aluminum, nickel, zinc, platinum, gold, and asbestos) has tripled since 1940. Newly discovered oil fields provide 40 times as much "black gold" as in the days before World War II. Oil production has spurted from 21,000 barrels a day in 1946 to about 500,000 barrels a day in 1957.

Canada's vast iron ore deposits promise a steady supply of raw material for the manufacture of steel. And the Western Hemisphere's—and perhaps the entire world's—richest source of uranium (for atomic power) is located in the Canadian northland.

Industries in Wilderness

Factories north of the border are striving to keep pace with the exploitation of natural resources. Steel mills, oil refineries, aluminum smelters, and paper mills are springing up as if by magic. More than $7.5 billion was poured into expanding Canadian industry last year. Almost $1 billion of this investment came from U.S. sources.

Canadian government statistics underscore the impact of the economic boom. Industrial activity, employment, and national income keep hitting new highs. National production in 1956 jumped 11 per cent over the preceding year, to almost $30 billion. This figure is almost *four* times Canada's output in 1940! No other nation can even approach that record!

And the end is not yet in sight. An immense project has aroused enthusiasm in Canada's western prairielands. The construction of a $375 million natural gas pipeline—stretching from the western province of Alberta to eastern Canada—is nearing completion. This 2,200-mile-long pipeline—longest in the world —will provide fuel for the new factories springing up in wilderness areas, as well as for the established industries of Canada's more developed regions.

The most spectacular construction project of all—one in which the United States and Canada are working side by side—is the St. Lawrence Seaway. When the Seaway is finished in April 1959, ocean-going vessels will open up a new era of international commerce. For the first time, big ships will be able to sail up the St. Lawrence River to the Great Lakes. Such cities as Toronto and Chicago will become major ocean ports.

What has this meant to the average Canadian? He enjoys a standard of living rivaling that of his "Yankee" neighbor. What's more, many economists predict that Canadians soon may have the *highest* standard of living in the world—bar none! (One indicative sidelight: The U.S. dollar is worth only 97 cents north of the border!)

NATURAL RESOURCES AND ECONOMIC POTENTIAL [3]

Only one nation in the world, the Soviet Union, exceeds Canada in size. Only two or three possess untapped resources as bountiful as those of Canada. These two factors, plus a location facing three of the important oceans of the world and next door to the United States, plus membership in the British Commonwealth of Nations, have brought Canada to world prominence at mid-twentieth century.

Vastness, of course, has imposed burdens, particularly in the fields of transportation and communications. It has meant an extensive rather than an intensive use of the land. Although the population is now nearing the eighteen million mark, the over-all density is only a little more than four persons per square mile, compared, for instance, with 194 in France and 619 in Japan. But size and emptiness, combined with immense quantities of lumber, fuel, and metallic minerals are now beginning to pay off.

Canada's location on the great circle air routes across the Arctic between the major centers of North America, Europe, and the Soviet Union, has rendered it of ever-increasing strategic

[3] From *Canada*, pamphlet by Theo L. Hills, associate professor in the department of geography, McGill University. (Focus Series, vol 9, no5) American Geographical Society. New York. January 1959. p 1-6. Reprinted by permission.

importance internationally, as witness the series of early warning radar lines across its northern reaches—the DEW Line and the Mid-Canada Line. Its location fronting on both the Atlantic and Pacific oceans, and its common land border with a rich neighbor have multiplied opportunities for trade. . . . And through membership in the British Commonwealth, Canada has retained in Britain a large and reliable market for a variety of exports, and has benefited from preferential trade agreements throughout the Commonwealth. . . .

The Landscape

Canada is generally divided into several rather symmetrically arranged regions. In the heart of the country and occupying more than half of its expanse is the Canadian Shield. In the far north the Shield gives way to the scattered islands of the Arctic; to the west and east it is flanked by lowlands—to the west the Prairies and the Mackenzie Basin, to the east the Great Lakes-St. Lawrence lowland. Beyond these are the mountainous ocean borderlands . . . [in the west] and, in the east, the Appalachians.

The Shield . . . is an intensely glaciated plateau, formed of ancient and resistant rocks. The dense forests of spruce, tamarack, and birch, immensely rich metalliferous veins in its Pre-Cambrian rocks, and innumerable lakes acting as a huge reservoir for dozens of large rivers, have encouraged industrial development though as yet chiefly at the exploitative level. Infertile and acid soils, permanently frozen subsoil, severe winters, and a short growing season have militated against agricultural settlement. . . .

Commerce and industry

Canada is traditionally pictured as an agricultural country, but, actually, the activities that have given drive to the economy have been commercial and, more recently, industrial rather than agricultural. In turn, the codfish trade, the fur trade, the timber trade, the wheat trade, the pulp and paper and mineral trades have been the mainstay of the economy.

For the better part of a hundred years American industry has insisted upon taking Canadian products in raw or semi-processed form, and this is nowhere more obvious than in the forestry and mining industries (the large-scale manufacture of newsprint is the only exception). Not only does the United States provide by far the major market for the products of these industries, but United States capital has developed and today controls more than 50 per cent of their productive capacity.

The forest industries currently employ 5 per cent of the labor force and contribute 6 per cent of the value of the country's total revenue. Lumber, chiefly from British Columbia, and newsprint, chiefly from the east, especially Quebec, are the most important products, and 90 per cent of the newsprint (80 per cent to the United States) and 50 per cent of the lumber are exported. Canada's forests extend over an area of 1.5 million square miles and two thirds of them are commercial stands of timber. It is estimated that on a sustained yield basis production could be doubled on land now classed as accessible.

A fourfold increase in the last twenty years in the value of mineral production, which now is about $2,133 million [in Canadian dollars], expresses only partly the most spectacular advance in the economy. In 1957 raw or semi-processed minerals represented 30 per cent of all exports. Canada has long been the world's largest producer and exporter of nickel and asbestos, a place it is likely to hold well into the future. Petroleum output, the annual value of which is twice as great as that of any other mineral, is expanding rapidly, and will continue to do so; only a fraction of the Prairies potential has been tapped so far. Long-established centers and new discoveries, especially on the Shield and in British Columbia, have kept nickel, copper, zinc, lead, gold, iron ore, and uranium among the top-ranking minerals; the last two, in fact, are certain to outpace all but petroleum within a few years. Uranium production, for instance, tripled during 1957 with the inauguration of operations in big new mills in the Blind River area of Ontario and increased operations elsewhere.

Canada is today one of the world's leading manufacturers—probably the sixth largest. About 30 per cent of the national income is derived from manufacturing, mostly from pulp and paper, non-ferrous metal smelting and refining, petroleum products, food processing, and saw-milling, using domestic raw materials; and from machinery, motor vehicles, aircraft, rubber, textiles and clothing, and electrical apparatus, using chiefly imported raw or semi-manufactured materials.

All but six per cent of the manufactures are for home consumption. Ontario is the most industrialized province, producing annually about half of the manufactured goods, and all of the major industries are represented here, notably automobiles, agricultural implements, tobacco processing, and iron and steel. Quebec predominates in the pulp and paper, aluminum, textile and clothing, and railroad rolling stock industries. Manufacturing has spread rapidly in the postwar period in the Prairie provinces and British Columbia, but Montreal is still the prime industrial center, and Toronto runs a close second.

Canada has only just begun to exploit its energy potential—water power on the southern fringe of the Shield, in the St. Lawrence, and in the Western Cordillera, and the vast oil-bearing fields in the interior lowlands. Coal, 60 per cent of which is imported, largely from the United States, still provides almost half of the energy used by industry; electricity provides 24 per cent of it, and petroleum products 22 per cent.

The installed hydroelectric capacity of 20 million horsepower in 1958 is the second largest in the world, after the United States, but this is no more than one quarter of the recorded potential. Quebec, which has nearly half the installed capacity, relies on the power of the St. Lawrence and its north bank tributaries, especially the Ottawa, Saguenay, and St. Maurice. Ontario uses power chiefly from the St. Lawrence—Great Lakes system. The tremendous potential of British Columbia has been as yet scarcely touched, and that of Labrador likewise.

Canada imports more than half of its petroleum requirements. It is currently more economical in general to import crude Venezuelan or Middle Eastern oil for the eastern industries and export the western surplus to western and north-central United States. However, a growing pipeline system, particularly the recently completed transcontinental natural gas line, should before long bring large quantities of oil and natural gas to the east.

Nothing has done more to enable the country to consolidate its east-west link and withstand the economic pulls to the south than the 45,000 miles of railroad that span the continent and the new 5,000-mile Trans-Canada Highway now being built and scheduled for completion in 1961. But the most spectacular development in the transportation field in recent years, of course, has been the St. Lawrence Seaway, which . . . will provide cheap and quick transport from the Atlantic to Lake Superior through the elimination of the shipping bottleneck above Montreal and the dredging of all channels to a depth of 27 feet. It is estimated that four fifths of the Seaway traffic will be bulk raw materials, such as iron ore from the Labrador-Quebec area to the Great Lakes steel centers. [See "Meaning for Labrador's Ore" in this section, below.] Aviation, too, is greatly aiding in the development of the economy as a whole and the penetration of the Arctic region and exploration of its mineral resources.

Farming and Fishing

Altogether agriculture contributes about 13 per cent of the national income and employs 15 per cent of the labor force. In the last twenty years the volume of farm production has increased by more than 50 per cent, though the area of improved land increased by only 11 million acres, from 86 million to 97 million. This has been achieved mainly by a very great rise in the productivity per acre as a result of a mechanical revolution, abandonment of land of poor quality, development of disease-resistant grain crops, and expansion of irrigation and of the acreage devoted to high-value specialty crops such as sugar beets and tobacco.

Wheat still reigns supreme among Canadian grains. In fact, on August 1, 1957, the beginning of the crop year, the carryover of wheat reached the unprecedented total of 723 million bushels, largely because of six years of bumper harvests. Elevators were also jammed to capacity with an additional 385 million bushels of oats, barley, rye, and flaxseed. This surplus problem, a serious one for Canada, is aggravated by a surplus in the United States, and that country's surplus program. But the specialized wheat economy of the Prairies is slowly being replaced by a more diversified cultivation, and the raising of livestock. Dairy production has expanded as rapidly here as elsewhere in the country, and, in addition, the Prairies today have become the country's main source of beef cattle.

Agriculture in the Western Cordillera is characterized by a pronounced regional specialization—stone fruit and apples in the Okanogan Valley, dairying and truck farming in the lower Fraser Valley, for example—a reflection of the broken terrain and varied climates.

In the east, livestock have become by far the largest source of income to the farmers. A federal freight assistance program has aided this trend by increasing consumption of feed grain shipped from the west, for livestock depends more on fodder crops here than on pasture. The other striking development in the east is an increasing diversification resulting from the exploitation of special soil and climatic conditions, such as tobacco in Norfolk County (Ontario) and Joliette (Quebec); potatoes on Prince Edward Island; fruit, especially apples and peaches, in the Niagara and St. Lawrence lowlands; and truck farming in southern Ontario and around Montreal

Fishing continues to play a significant role in the Canadian economy. The landing of some two billion pounds of fish each year provides the livelihood of about eighty thousand people and large quantities of fish for export. The modernized Atlantic fisheries, specializing in lobster, cod, haddock, and halibut, contribute more than half of the total catch by value. The Pacific fisheries concentrate on salmon, halibut, and herring. Protection afforded to the salmon industry by United States-Canadian cooperation is paying great dividends.

The People

Economists are constantly debating the question of whether or not Canada needs more people. Some of them would like to see a population of 30 million by 1975. In the long run, it would seem that the country will need additional manpower if it is to develop more fully its natural resources and industry, and much of this will have to come from abroad, for the natural rate of growth is not high. [See Section V for a fuller discussion of population growth and immigration policy.]

Although the traditional conflict between an industrial and urban east and an agricultural west has diminished, regional disparities remain. The chief problem is the Atlantic provinces, which lack the wide resource base of the rest of the country. The question is how far should federal aid be extended to them. Indeed, many Canadians question the wisdom of speeding up the tempo of exploitation in general, especially if it means further United States capital investment. How far, they ask, should continental integration be carried? Perhaps it is inevitable. In any case, whatever the methods used, the potential wealth is there, the pattern of development seems to be well established, and the economic stride will undoubtedly continue to be a vigorous one.

THE ST. LAWRENCE SEAWAY: WHAT IT IS AND WHAT IT MEANS [4]

The troubles of the St. Lawrence River, one of the great waterways of the world, are about to come to an end. . . . [On July 1, 1958] thirty tons of dynamite, scattered through the deep earthen walls of a coffer dam upstream of the big new Barnhart Island dam and powerhouse, . . . [ripped] away the temporary dam and let the St. Lawrence move back into her old, accustomed channel. There she will . . . work, making electricity for New York State and Vermont and the Province of Ontario, and offering new deep-water ship channels for the commerce of the world to pass to and from the inland seaports of the United States and Canada.

What The Seaway Is

Just as the Seaway is a joint venture of two great nations, so it is a joint venture of shipping and hydroelectric power. It is a kind of marriage of convenience because the waters of the St. Lawrence must serve two purposes—to float cargoes and a few

[4] From "What The Seaway Is," feature article by Paul J. C. Friedlander, special correspondent for the New York *Times*. Section 11, p 1. June 29, 1958. Reprinted by permission.

passengers along what is sometimes called the fourth coast of this continent, and to spin the turbines that spin the generators that create electricity that will, beginning in September, light homes and power factories from the southern reaches of the Catskill Mountains to the northerly frontiers of Ontario.

The St. Lawrence Seaway and Power Project is so big that it took four governmental agencies to put it together. The power project was built cooperatively by the New York State Power Authority and the Ontario Hydro-Electric Power Commission. The New York Power Authority was established as a nonprofit authority by the State of New York and committed to build and operate the St. Lawrence power project and another just getting started at Niagara Falls. Ontario Hydro-Electric is the long-established provincial government unit that furnishes electric power to the entire Province of Ontario. Each built, paid for and owns half of the power dam and each will get, to the kilo-watt, the same amount of electricity.

Twin Administrations. The shipping project has two counter-parts, also. The United States part of the work is owned and operated by the St. Lawrence Seaway Development Corporation of the United States, a Government agency created by Congress. For Canada the agency is the St. Lawrence Seaway Authority of Canada. And for the benefit of those pessimists who do not believe that nations may work together as nations and people as people across borders and frontiers, the word the length of the Seaway is that they can. From the top brass down through the engineers, from the power shovel operators down to the few shovel-stiffs used on the project, the four authorities produced a maximum of cooperation and a minimum of disagreement.

The difficulty when speaking or writing of the Seaway, and it will probably be true also for the millions of people expected to make their way . . . in the years to come to the banks of the St. Lawrence River, its locks and its dams, is that it is so spread out that it literally prohibts a short, compact description. Fur-thermore, it is like an iceberg, with most of its physical com-ponents underground or underwater; what remains visible is deceptive. Only the construction workers, and a few lucky ob-servers, know its overbearing size. . . .

To say that the Seaway project consists of seven new locks, 800 feet long and eighty feet wide, capable of handling ships of twenty-seven-foot draft, of new channels dredged to carry the twenty-seven-foot vessels; that it comprises three new dams, the Barnhart Island Dam and powerhouse, the Long Sault Dam that forces the river to pile up behind the powerhouse gates, and the Iroquois Dam that helps control the river flow forty-odd miles upstream; that it will cost one billion dollars, and that it will create electricity with the power of 2.1 million horses, and let bigger ships sail from the ocean to the furthermost Great Lakes —these are factual understatements. Euclid to the contrary, here the whole is greater than the sum of all of its parts.

What the Seaway Means

The Seaway means electric power for industries and for commercial and residential use in vast areas on both sides of the international border that have been short of power. The booming growth of industry throughout the open spaces of Ontario is threatening to burn up every kilowatt of power Ontario-Hydro's stations can produce. The demand is so widespread that the new St. Lawrence power is to be fed into the grid of high-tension lines feeding the province to bolster up the power throughout the territory. There is no electricity shortage yet, but the rate of growth for both the population and industry is so head-long that Barnhart power will soon be only a stop-gap.

On the United States side of the river the power will make it possible for industry to grow in the rural northeastern corner of New York State and for Vermont to feed its homes and its factories with electricity. Not all the industries, municipal electric distribution systems and rural cooperatives to be serviced by the State Power Authority have been without power or seriously short of it.

The advantage they will gain from state power will be its lower cost, which must be passed on to the consumer. St. Lawrence power will run about 25 per cent less than present wholesale rates. Since transmission costs will remain constant, the ultimate cost of electricity to the retail consumer in factory or home is expected to run about 10 per cent less than it costs now from private utilities.

Industrial and economic developments are expected not only from expansion because of the new power supply but also because of the effects of deep-water shipping on a vast sweep of the continent that touches on great industrial centers of both Canada and the United States. One of the major inducements for building the Seaway was the discovery and development of high-grade Labrador iron ores. Ore fields in the Midwest that have been supplying the steel mills of Pennsylvania, Ohio, Indiana, New York State and Ontario have begun to wear thin.

Some steel mills ringing the Great Lakes have considered moving their plants to Atlantic coast ports to be near deep-water ore carriers. The Seaway after . . . April 1 [1959] will bring deep-water ore carriers right up to the river to Great Lakes ports that are already expanding their harbor facilities and adding to their peripheral highways to improve trucking between ore boats and blast furnaces.

There is bound to be a shuffling along the lakes and on the river as new and larger grain boats take to the enlarged locks and canals, carrying the harvest from the prairie states down to Montreal and on out to sea and to farflung world markets without costly and time-consuming transshipping at Prescott, Ontario, into small boats for Montreal, and at Montreal into big ships for ocean crossings.

Profits and Losses. There is bound to be, also, expansion, changes, gains and, perhaps in some cases, losses, in jobs, in markets, in plants and in distribution of consumer goods as, in the years ahead, the effects of the Seaway begin to be felt in almost every segment of the economy of the northeastern half of Canada and the United States.

Two examples will suffice: Shipyards on the lakes are busy now building new big "lakers" to fit the large-size locks and the demand for big cargo carriers. Shippers as far from each other as Montreal and New Orleans, and all the lakefront and riverside industries in between are trying now to figure out where their new markets will be and how best to exploit them when connecting waterways are completed and freight will move freely from the Gulf of Mexico up the Mississippi River to the Great Lakes, and from the North Atlantic up the St. Lawrence River and the lakes and thence down to Mississippi River ports.

The Job of Construction

The St. Lawrence Seaway and Power Project is so big that it was built in several separate, sometimes remote, sections. . . .

For four years thousands of men, as many as 6,000 at a time on a single aspect of the project, (the over-all peak was 22,000) and hundreds of different pieces of giant machinery, some shipped over from England and France for the duration of the job, hauled and pushed the St. Lawrence River around. They dammed the waters here and sent them circling somewhere else so they could scrape the river bed clear down to bedrock and pour their concrete barricades and build their giant ship locks. They dredged new channels and old, they gouged out her banks here and filled them in there to straighten the waterway and smooth the flow of troubled waters. . . .

Seaway's History

The dream of a passage around the rapids of the St. Lawrence so men could move freely between the river's mouth and the inland seas where its waters rise has occupied occupants of this continent for centuries. The Indians rode the rapids in their war canoes; this was the warpath of the Iroquois when they plunged down across a border that did not exist until the white men came, and fought with the tribes of New York State and New England. The first attempt to build a canal—a shallow thing deep enough only to float a canoe—was reported in the early eighteenth century.

When the white explorers first probed this part of the New World they were searching for a Northwest Passage to the riches of India and the Orient, the counterpart of the passage that Columbus failed to find.

In later years St. Lawrence passage became more important to Canada than to the United States, and the canals and locks that have been in use . . . [up to June 1958] were on the Canadian side of the international border. Agitation for construction of the Seaway started in Canada and was resisted for years by Congress. Not until Canada threatened to go ahead on her own and build a new seaway all on the Canadian side of the river was it possible to move Congress to act. There is considerable debate, whenever the Seaway's shipping and power men get together, as to which is more important, and which came first, power or shipping.

The power people argue that power—via the power dam, the water control dams and dredging essential to insure their flow of water—is paying a larger share of the total cost than is shipping, and that if power had not found it feasible to build a hydroelectric station on the river, the shipping part could not have been built with any sense of economics. Seaway tolls are designed to pay for the shipping parts of the project in fifty years. The power facilities on the Canadian side are Government-owned, but the New York Power Authority sold bonds to raise its funds, also repaying on a fifty-year retirement basis. . . .

Like all great projects, the Seaway, born in controversy over shipping and power, is likely to continue to the end of its days with its worth, its benefits, its advantages and disadvantages always being weighed and debated.

Meanwhile, electricity will flow through high wires and low, the ships will move their freight, and the St. Lawrence River will continue to move from the Great Lakes to the sea in all its gentle majesty.

THE MEANING FOR CANADIAN PORTS [5]

The great power project, which will pump desperately needed electricity into the industrial complexes of power-starved Ontario, has grabbed most of the seaway headlines. But . . . [Canada] has made it clear that . . . the navigation side of the project [is] just as important as its power potential. Canadians expect that the seaway will pour $100 million a year into its economy.

[5] From "Canada's Seaway Empire," news story. Newsweek. 40:77-9. August 6, 1956. Reprinted by permission.

Canadian enthusiasm for the seaway, while no less real than in the United States, is a bit more tempered. Reason: It must be measured against the background of the country's already surging economy. Oil in Canada's western prairies, the uranium strikes that made Saskatchewan another Klondike, the rich and apparently limitless iron ore deposits now being worked in Labrador—these have given Canada's sixteen million people one bonanza after another. "So many breath-taking things are happening," a businessman explained, "that we're numb. It's like a kind of shell shock."

Nonetheless, from Montreal to Fort William and Port Arthur at the head of Lake Superior, Canada's cities are dreaming dreams of ocean trade and brandishing boasts and blueprints as they talk of new glory as ocean ports. This intense rivalry is at its hottest in eastern Canada's three top inland ports—Montreal on the St. Lawrence and Toronto and Hamilton on Lake Ontario.

When Louis XIV gave Montreal to the Company of New France in the middle of the seventeenth century, the harbor was a towpath along the waterfront; now it is one of the busiest inland ports in the world. The $73 million man-made harbor stretches some sixteen miles along the south edge of the Island of Montreal—10 miles of wharfs, with more than a hundred berths, twenty seven transit sheds, four grain elevators, a cold-storage warehouse, heavy-lift equipment, and ship repair yards. Besides the fleets of "lakers," 1,700 ocean-going ships use Montreal harbor every year. A busy day sees a vessel moving in or out every twenty-five minutes.

The first ocean freighter that noses into the 27-foot channels of the upper St. Lawrence in 1959 will end Montreal's near monopoly on blue-water shipping for eastern Canada. At first, Montrealers had depressing visions of disconsolate citizens standing on the docks waving sadly at ships sailing past on their way to Toronto. . . . That mood has disappeared like river ice in the spring. Montreal's citizens are convinced that their port will stay the biggest in Canada—and get bigger as traffic grows. To back up that conviction, they are gambling another $12 million on harbor facilities.

The argument for optimism runs this way: Two thirds of Montreal's shipping business now is with its own hinterland. The seaway won't hurt this. Instead, it will probably increase as the Canadian boom rolls on and as Quebec industry builds up.

Most of the rest of the city's shipping business is grain— and here the seaway will prove a real help. Grain now moves down the lakes to Prescott and other Ontario ports where it is transshipped from the big lakers to "canallers," small enough to navigate the present 14-foot seaway channels and canals. At Montreal, the grain has to be shifted again, this time into ocean bottoms. When the seaway is dredged, the lakers can make the run all the way to Montreal. Cutting out the time and money needed for the Lake Ontario transfer to canallers, grain shippers can save as much as 5 or 6 cents a bushel.

The grain trade looms largest in Montreal's plans. George S. Mooney, director of the city's St. Lawrence Municipal Bureau, calls it "the immediate and compelling justification for the seaway." "No responsible and informed authority that I know of," Mooney sums up, "has any doubts that the port and harbor of Montreal will continue to be Canada's greatest port and that grain will continue to be its chief export commodity."

Two centuries ago, a French man-o'-war laden with trade goods consigned to the Keeper of the Port carried the first cargo into the harbor of Toronto. Today, more than four thousand ships, in both coastwise and international trade, move through the port each year, carrying 4.5 million tons of cargo. Last year, twenty overseas lines—with a fleet of 110 ships—showed their flags at Toronto for a total of 792 overseas entrances and clearances.

Some 300 miles west of Montreal, Toronto is sprucing up its busy waterfront for a seaway boom. Here general cargo (the high-priced stuff in barrels and boxes), rather than grain, is king. The city is the gateway to Canada's greatest concentration of population and industry (some 4,400 factories producing 157 groups of products). From Toronto, a road and rail net spreads across the dominion. Three hundred freight and passenger trains and 3,200 trucks move in and out daily. The port facilities are big and efficient. All this, Torontonians are convinced, will be a magnet for the new ocean cargoes the seaway will bring.

Signs have already appeared that the magnet has begun its work even before the seaway opens. One European line has let it be known that it stands ready to lose $50,000 a year for five years, just to be sure of a place on the waterfront.

E. B. Griffith, the port's general manager, and the city's energetic Port Commission are readying things for these eager clients. The city has built a 100,000-square-foot terminal for ocean freight and a 3,300-foot dock that sprawls over 26 acres. A new open berth and four more terminals are on the drawing-boards. Toronto port experts figure that shippers will concentrate on one port rather than try to spread one cargo over half-a-dozen stops. And, of course, they are betting that Toronto will be the one big stop.

Like most Canadians, Torontonians keep a checkrein on their enthusiasm. "With the expanding economy and lower transportation costs," says port manager Griffith, "we may expect a solid substantial increase in trade—but don't expect everyone in Toronto to be a millionaire in twenty years." Despite this restraint, Toronto's citizens are sure that the seaway will be the biggest thing for their port since that man-o'-war cleared their harbor 200 years ago and they ignore loud threats of competition from their smaller rival to the southwest, Hamilton, "Hamilton," said one, "is a dirty word in Toronto."

When Edward Acraman designed a coat of arms for the newly incorporated city of Hamilton in 1947, he gave prominent place to "a British steamer, schooner rigged, as the most expeditious modern mode of commercial intercourse." Acraman was giving a well-earned nod to Hamilton's magnificent harbor, "the finest on the Lakes," according to the steel city's boosters. . . . [In 1955] more than 7.5 million tons passed through the port, topped in Canada only by Montreal and the Pacific Coast's Vancouver. Nineteen foreign ship lines now call at Hamilton.

To back up their bitter rivalry with Toronto, Hamiltonians point proudly to the advantages of their port: It's both bigger and more accessible than Toronto's. Hamilton's factories (two of Canada's biggest steel producers, 500 other industries) stand on its waterfront. In Toronto, the business and financial districts fence off industry from the docks. Toronto boasts better rail facilities, but Hamilton claims better roads (and is hotly disputed by its neighbor). Toronto, of course, has the obvious advantage of size (Hamilton's population is 210,000 against Toronto's 1.1 million), but the smaller city thinks it can become the shipping center for the cluster of other manufacturing towns around it: Brantford, Oakville, Kitchener, Guelph, London, Niagara Falls, St. Catharines.

Even the boosters admit one serious flaw: Hamilton's dock and port facilities are inadequate and outdated. The "Ambitious City" figures that few of the big ships that will use the seaway will go beyond the Toronto-Hamilton area on the Canadian side and the port with the best transshipment facilities will win out. To improve its chances, Hamilton's harbor commissioners are working overtime on new docks, warehouses, and cargo-handling equipment, at a cost of $1 million a year.

The claims and counterclaims echo in every Great Lakes port. In a characteristic understatement, [President of Canada's St. Lawrence Seaway Authority] Chevrier has pointed out: "The seaway will have tremendous influence on every part of Canada and certainly on the heartland of America." With the new waterway, he said, "we will have changed the geography of the St. Lawrence Valley, but even more radically we will have changed its whole economic structure." From Belle Isle to Montreal, from Buffalo to Chicago, businessmen are figuring ways and means to win their share of the new commerce these changes will create. The dream is moving off the blueprints into the balance sheets.

[The St. Lawrence Seaway opened unofficially in the last week of April 1959 with the passage of two Canadian icebreakers through the system of locks to the Great Lakes. The first ocean-going ship behind the icebreakers was a Dutch freighter.—Ed.]

THE MEANING FOR LABRADOR'S ORE [6]

Of all the industries and groups anticipating big benefits from the opening of the St. Lawrence Seaway, the United States steel industry has the highest hopes and perhaps the most justification

[6] From "Labrador's Ore to Aid Seaway," feature article by Clark Davey, New York *Times* correspondent. New York *Times*. Section 11, p 16. June 29, 1958. Reprinted by permission.

for them. The most informed estimates predict that the rich iron ore from the barely tapped ore fields of Quebec and Labrador will constitute at least 30 per cent of the entire Seaway traffic. In the first five years ore shipments are expected to average 10 million tons annually.

Before the end of the second five-year period, this total will have increased, it is expected, to close to 20 million tons a year. The first figure represents about 30 per cent of the total traffic in those years and the second figure better than 40 per cent.

In fact, the success of the Seaway as a self-sustaining public utility in both Canada and the United States—both countries expect it to pay for itself in fifty years—may depend largely on iron ore.

As such, ore could well be the major factor controlling the establishing and the eventual revision of the rates of tolls charged on all bulk cargoes. The administrators of the Seaway must maintain a toll rate that will attract the maximum tonnage of iron ore.

It is also true that the steel-makers of the Midwest provided the final support that made United States participation in the project a certainty. This support did not materialize, however, until the Quebec-Labrador deposits of ore were developed beginning in 1949.

Naturally, because any toll represents an added charge on ore and an increase in the cost of production, the steel makers have carried on a continuing but unsuccessful campaign to have the Seaway operated as a free way. Canada's largest steel producer, the Steel Company of Canada, Ltd., at Hamilton, has estimated that a toll of 50 cents a ton on both its coal and ore—and the estimated bulk toll is close to that figure—would increase the cost of making a ton of steel by 85 cents.

But what the steel makers—Canadian and American—have not estimated is the saving created by the Seaway. Obviously if 20 million tons are to be moved through the seven locks and channels of the system, the route must be cheaper than delivering the Quebec-Labrador ore to points close to Baltimore on the Atlantic Coast for transshipment to the mills of Pittsburgh or even, by rail, to the Ohio mills. And the Seaway route must be cheaper even after tolls are applied or the ore simply will move over other competitive routes.

However, there is increasing evidence that the Great Lakes mills need the Quebec-Labrador ore. Minnesota's Mesabi range reserves are not limitless and the Canadian ore represents the next closest supply.

The reserves in what is known as the Labrador trough are tremendous and can be estimated only in the billions of tons. Recently Canada's Minister of Natural Resources, Alvin Hamilton, told a parliamentary committee that the reserves on Baffin Island may be greater than any yet uncovered on the continent.

United States firms have invested heavily in the development of Labrador ore. More than $300 million was spent in the area before the first ton of ore was shipped. Two companies, the Iron Ore Company of Canada—controlled by the Hanna interests —and Quebec-Cartier are both building concentrators which will produce, between them, sometime in the early 1960's, about 16 million tons of concentrate, grading 65-66 per cent iron.

This concentration process is expected to increase the value of the Seaway since the tolls will be levied against a higher-value ore. As a result, it seems likely that these concentrates will move largely through the Seaway, with a tendency to keep direct-shipping ores moving to East Coast points.

There have been suggestions that at least one major steel interest—that controlled by Cyrus Eaton—will try to beat Seaway tolls by establishing a big steel plant at or near Contrecoeur on the south shore of the St. Lawrence River, twenty-five miles east of Montreal. Contrecoeur, as the major transshipment point for Quebec-Labrador ore moving by rail into Pittsburgh and other United States mills, is already equipped with the most modern ore-handling facilities.

There have long been rumors that the Eaton interests will link with European capital—the most likely prospects are the Krupps of Germany—to funnel Ungava ore in which they have a mutual interest.

One Canadian firm, the Dominion Steel and Coal Corporation now controlled by the A. V. Roe Canada group, has already revealed that it will build a fabricating plant near Contrecoeur which, for the time being, will get its basic steel from the company's operation at Sydney, Nova Scotia.

Another factor which must be considered is the announced intention of the relatively new Canadian Government of encouraging the processing of a much higher percentage of Canada's natural resources in this country.

During his . . . [1958] election campaign, Prime Minister John G. Diefenbaker came close to calling the Seaway a folly because it would be funneling the richness of the Quebec-Labrador ore into United States blast furnaces. How his Government hopes to change this particular situation remains to be seen. Many observers feel that the Government will not be able to make any substantial change on the movement of ore through the Seaway. The same observers believe that the conveyor belt metaphor is as good as any to apply to the Seaway as far as the Midwest United States steel industry is concerned.

THE ARCTIC POTENTIAL [7]

Some scientists estimate that the polar ice pack is 40 per cent thinner and 12 per cent less in area than it was a half-century ago, and that even within the lifetime of our children the Arctic Ocean may open, enabling ships to sail over the North Pole, as the submarines Nautilus and Skate recently sailed under it. A ship bound from New York to Tokyo would save 2,500 miles by turning left outside the Narrows and sailing past Greenland instead of through the Panama Canal.

Regardless of climate trends, the Arctic is changing in other ways. The traditional life of the Eskimos is doomed. Last winter, a score or more starved because of depopulation of their food source, the caribou. Civilization is invading the trackless tundra and even the inhospitable ice of the Arctic Ocean. Military installations—such as the Distant Early Warning radar net, or DEW Line, across the American Arctic—have been built on both sides of the Pole. As part of the International Geophysical

[7] From "The Changing Face of the Arctic," by Walter Sullivan, of New York *Times* staff. New York *Times Magazine*. p28+. October 19, 1958. Reprinted by permission.

Year, the Soviet Union and the United States are each maintaining two research stations on drifting ice.

More than anything else, it is the airplane that has doomed the isolation of the Arctic. Until recent decades the region lay beyond the reach of all outsiders except for the hardiest explorers. Now prospectors and hunters fly in in search of wealth or sport. Regularly scheduled airliners stop at Point Barrow, Barter Island and similar outposts on the shores of the Arctic Ocean, and dainty ladies sip champagne above the North Pole on intercontinental flights. Civilization is closing about the top of the world like a tightening noose.

The Sea and Land

Strangely, there is no generally accepted definition of what the Arctic is. Some say it begins at the Arctic Circle, where one enters the land of the midnight sun. But this arbitrary line excludes Iceland and a considerable part of Greenland.

Some say the Arctic begins where the trees end, yet the tree line is whimsical. Although most of northern Canada is treeless, spruces extend virtually to the Arctic Ocean along great rivers like the Mackenzie.

The broadest definition is that the Arctic is the region of permafrost, or permanently frozen subsoil. In other latitudes, the ground is unfrozen except when it congeals to a depth of a foot or two in winter. In the permafrost region, the reverse is true. Ground and bedrock are frozen to depths of a thousand feet or more, with only a shallow thaw in summer. By the criterion of permafrost, almost half of the Soviet Union, half of Canada and a large part of Alaska belong to the Arctic.

Although the idea that a solid ice sheet covers the central Arctic has lingered stubbornly in the popular fancy, the northern cap of ice worn by our planet is actually a thin crust—on the whole, only about seven feet thick—over an ocean two miles deep in places.

Known as the pack, this ice is constantly shifting, splitting, changing. The sea upon which it rides is bounded by the northern coast of Europe, Asia and North America—vast stretches of tundra (where no trees are able to grow) and taiga (where the trees are stunted).

The only major land-borne ice sheet in the north covers Greenland. Such is the weight of the Greenland ice that the island has sunk into the plastic underlayers of the earth until its center is now below sea level, under ten thousand feet of ice. There are scattered, smaller ice caps in the Arctic, but most of Siberia, Alaska and northern Canada is ice-free.

The Arctic is a region of wild contrasts: silence and crashing sound, darkness and light, sterile snow and lush vegetation.

The pack can be congealed into one seemingly unbroken crust—white, pinnacled, hummocked, glistening and silent. Yet it is forever moving over the sea and, when torn by wind or obstructing land, it splits, shrieking and grinding, into floes that override one another or form lofty pressure ridges.

In the vicinity of the Pole, day lasts six months, and darkness or twilight an equal time. Yet, because the warmth carried north by ocean currents leaks out through the ice into the atmosphere, winter at the North Pole is not much colder than in North Dakota, where 44 degrees below zero has been recorded. The lowest temperature last winter at Drifting Station A, one of the American research bases on a floe near the Pole, was minus 56.9 degrees. Snowfall in the North Pole area, in an entire year, is said to be less than that of an Illinois winter. Except for mountaintops or areas refrigerated by nearby ice, there are few places in the Arctic where the mercury does not rise to 80 degrees in summer.

When the sun returns after the long night, the Arctic comes to life with a rush. The snows that cover the tundra dissolve among carpets of flowers that burst into bloom with dazzling brilliance.

The permafrost keeps surface water from draining into the ground, with the result that from the air one sees the vast sweep of lake-speckled tundra glisten as though completely flooded. On foot, one may sink to the knees in moss and grass. Yet there are also arid or rocky sections of the Arctic, impressive for their black-and-white starkness rather than for their verdancy.

Arctic Animals

The North teems with animal life. None is more fascinating than the lemmings. These mouselike creatures multiply, at the rate of several litters a season, until the tundra seems alive with them. Then, having nibbled the tundra clean of food, they migrate, apparently in quest of new pastures. An army of predators pursues them—foxes, wolves, owls, ermine and rapacious gulls, with spearlike tails, called jaegers. Swimming across all water obstacles, some lemmings reach the Arctic Ocean and plunge in, seemingly in ignorance of its width.

The tundra remains webbed with the criss-crossing galleries which the lemmings bored through the grass in their quest for food beneath the winter snow. The ground is littered with pellets resembling black golf balls. Each is the undigested remains of a lemming, regurgitated by the white owl that ate it. But hardly a lemming is seen until the pastures recover and a new cycle begins.

The Arctic mountains harbor such fierce inhabitants as the barren-ground grizzly, the bane of DEW Line campers. Food caches have been completely devoured, the bears systematically biting into each can and sucking out the contents. In one case, a bear sampled some gasoline cans, as well as a box of smoke bombs, one of which went off. In the ensuing chaos, the bear tore a tent to ribbons and hurled crates for fifty yards in all directions.

In the passes leading to the Arctic slope, wolves lie in wait for the flowing rivers of caribou, migrating northward for the summer. Occasionally a loping wolverine, pausing every few dozen yards to rise on his hind feet like an elongated raccoon, comes down from the mountains. Although smaller than a wolf, he is so ferocious that he will drive a whole pack from their kill.

At first glance, the Arctic Ocean and its ice would seem a totally impossible habitat for land animals. But polar bears, made ravenous by the winter shortage of seals, have been seen on floes hundreds of miles from land, and have even been known to swim twenty or thirty miles of open ocean.

On one occasion during the past winter night, a supply plane from Alaska was approaching Drifting Station A, which has a landing strip on the ice. The ground crew threw the switch to turn on the runway lights. Nothing happened. A polar bear had systematically gone up one side of the runway and down the other, swatting each light with its paw. The freshness of its tracks indicated that the bear was lurking near-by in the darkness, so the men hurried back to camp for weapons before making repairs, which they completed in the nick of time.

Arctic People

The human beings who, from the dawn of history, have inhabited the Arctic have long impressed their fellow men by their fortitude. Among technicians along the DEW Line one finds deep respect for the Eskimos. Gaiety and ingenuity seem to be their salient characteristics.

The Eskimos range from Greenland, across Canada and Alaska to eastern Siberia. Farther west, in the Eurasian Arctic, live the Chukchi, Nentsi and Lapps, likewise traditionally dependent on hunting, reindeer herding and fishing.

It can be said that the white man has brought his two greatest scourges to the people of the North: disease and money. Lacking resistance, the Eskimos, Aleuts and other northern groups have been hard hit by tuberculosis and venereal disease. Often young men and women have died before they could raise their children to self-sufficiency.

Today, the introduction of money is bringing about a social and economic revolution. Supplies for some DEW Line stations have to be hauled in on tractor-drawn sleds. The Eskimos have proved highly competent as 'cat-skinners," keeping the tractor-trains going in the subzero cold of the winter night. After weeks on the trail, their pay, including overtime, is substantial even by the standards of skilled workers in more temperate climes. Some are reputed to make well over $10,000 a year.

The impact on the Eskimo villages has been profound. Some tribes still use igloos and many Eskimo homes are little more than shacks of unpainted wood. The inevitable huskies are staked, howling, on near-by humps of tundra. Strings of fish hang drying in the sun. Yet the interiors of some of these houses are said to boast twenty-four-inch television sets and other glossy appliances.

Of course, there is no electric current, much less a television station. These items have been ordered from a mail-order catalogue, presumably for their prestige value.

Changing ways are particularly noticeable among the younger generation. Teen-age Eskimo girls still wear the hooded, fur-trimmed jackets of their ancestors, but often the legs beneath are clothed in bluejeans and bobby socks.

Despite the temptation of the white man's wages, most Eskimos still depend for their living on the hunt, and in summer, driven by the seasonal urgency that impels all life in the Arctic, Eskimo families work in shifts, hunting around the clock. The men's walrus-hide boats, or umiaks, are likely to be propelled by the latest in outboard motors. The spear has been replaced by the rifle.

Despite Eskimo skill in the hunt, the growing scarcity of caribou has faced some villages with starvation. It is estimated that only 300,000 caribou are left in all of Canada, and some villages are unable to intercept herds. In the past year, aircraft have been used to spot the animals and airlift entire villages to within range of their traditional game.

Tragedy also has beset some Eskimo villages where mineral deposits were exploited. In adapting themselves to an industrial civilization, the natives forgot their ancient skills, and when the mines closed suddenly the Eskimos found they were no longer able to live off the land.

The Arctic Potential

Why has the white man been moving so insistently into the Arctic? There are three main reasons: (1) Military strategy. (2) The need for natural resources. (3) The quest for knowledge.

From ancient times until comparatively recently the world's most strategic body of water was the Mediterranean—the center between East and West. The long-range bomber and the missile have transferred primary importance to the Arctic Ocean. The

shortest routes to the targets of Russia and America lie across—
or from—the top of the world. Airbases and radar nets of both
sides ring the Far North.

The expansion of the world's population and the shrinkage
of its resources have driven men to exploit the Arctic's possibilities. Because so much of the Soviet Union's territory lies
within the Arctic, the Russians have given special emphasis to its
development. Significantly, the first nuclear-powered ship to be
built by the Russians is an icebreaker which can help to keep
open the approaches to three of the world's greatest rivers: the
Ob, Yenisei and Lena.

To increase food output, the Russians have been pushing
their grain fields ever northward. They have even sought by
such means as sprinkling the countryside with coal dust to induce
early melting of the snow and thus achieve a longer growing
season.

In fact, it has been found that cold winters do not, in themselves, rule out the growing of grain, and the cultivation of
wheat, barley, oats and rye has been reported in the coldest
district of Siberia, near Yakutsk.

Prospecting in the Arctic has reached the stage where at least
some of the resources are known. The coal which turns the industries of Leningrad is said to come from the mines near Vor-
kuta, north of the Arctic Circle. Lead is mined in Greenland.
The coal of Spitzbergen is of high quality. Coal and oil along
the north coast of Alaska only await the day when local transport
or industry justifies their exploitation. The great Ungava iron
deposits now being developed in the Canadian sub-Arctic are an
indication that similar resources may be found further north.
Gold and uranium are mined on the fringes of the Arctic.

Two highways to the Arctic Ocean are being planned. One
would cross the oil-rich Peel Plateau of the Yukon and reach the
ocean west of the Mackenzie River delta. The other would pass
by the east end of Great Slave Lake, said to harbor the world's
greatest deposits of lead and zinc, reaching the ocean at Copper-
mine, 500 miles east of the Mackenzie.

The quest for knowledge has been intensified by the International Geophysical Year. The IGY scientists' attempts to clarify
the mechanics of the ice-age cycle may hold vast portent for the

future. If, as some speculate, the Arctic ice pack eventually melts, Hudson Bay and the great north-flowing rivers of Canada and the Soviet Union will be opened to world shipping, with momentous effects on the economies of those nations.

But, according to the most recent and widely discussed theory, the removal of the ice cover on the Arctic Ocean would saturate the now dry polar air, creating moist winds that would cascade such heavy snows on Canada and Eurasia as to bring a new ice age.

Even with the ice pack, others argue, cargo submarines could ply a route under the floes between Atlantic and Pacific. The voyage of the Nautilus was hailed by President Eisenhower as blazing such a trail. Perhaps his statement was intended to de-emphasize the military aspects of the trip, but it did not precipitate any scramble to build cargo subs which, in addition to being extremely expensive, would have to follow a route periled by shoals near the Bering Sea.

The immediate future in Arctic waters seems to belong to nuclear-powered military submarines, prowling safe from detection beneath the pack. Equipped to seek out open water, they can surface in channels and ponds among the floes to fire their deadly missiles.

Meanwhile, new radars are being developed, capable of warning against ballistic missiles, as the DEW Line is not. Their prospective locations are secret, but we may be sure they will be in the Far North.

In peace or war, whether it becomes warmer or even colder, the Arctic seems bound to be progressively engulfed by civilization—as long as civilization endures.

CANADA'S SOCIAL NEEDS [8]

It is disturbing to find in Canada a twentieth-century version of the problems which haunted Britain after the industrial revolution: social disruption, overcrowded towns, relatively high figures for infant mortality and child neglect. The Canadian revolution has been rapid, covering some fifteen to twenty years, but it

[8] From "Canada's Social Conscience," news story. *Economist.* 185:504+. November 9, 1957. Reprinted by permission.

looks as if Canada's social conscience is lagging behind, so that some of the mistakes of the old industrial countries may be repeated in the new.

The Canadian attitude is easily understood. The economic depression of the thirties made a deep mental wound; it is a harsh country in which to lack food and fuel. The Canadians feel: "Let us make money quickly while the going is good. Social welfare is a political luxury we cannot afford. Look at the British and where it has landed them." This attitude fits in with the pioneer spirit, the strong belief that "self help" is the best way. It fits in, too, with the religious fundamentalists, notably in oil-rich Alberta, who believe that sickness and misfortune are sent by Providence as punishment and that the Lord's work must not be interfered with by too much assistance from the state. It fits in, too, with the ambitions of the real estate men, the financiers and the industrial technicians.

Nearly two thirds of Canada's 16 million people live in the towns. It is estimated that by 1980 there will be 26 million people of whom 80 per cent will be urban. Already there is overcrowding, and Canadians show considerable reluctance to tackle their slums. Only Toronto, St John's, Newfoundland, and St John, New Brunswick, have undertaken small slum clearance schemes paid for by public funds. Toronto in the last ten years has expanded more rapidly than any other city in the world. But the expansion has all been outwards, leaving the old city center untouched and derelict. In spite of the new skyscrapers, the modern elegance of Bloor Street and the shining new underground, areas like Cabbage Town in the middle of the city are squalid, decaying and overcrowded. In such areas live the casual, unskilled workers, the older men, the physically handicapped, and those who cannot save from low wages to meet the unemployment of the Canadian winter.

The outskirts of some of the new company towns are shockingly squalid. For instance a new uranium town is being built beside Elliot Lake in Ontario just north of the Great Lakes, and by the end of this year [1957] about fifteen thousand people will be established out there in the virgin forest. Houses are graded according to income and status; as in other company towns homes for high grade executives are built at "Snob Hills."

Meanwhile the old neighboring town of Blind River receives the less intelligent and skilled, the poor and the desperate, for whom new mining is a lure; houses are overcrowded, local social aid is strained, the liquor shops thrive and the jails are full.

Canada's rate of infant mortality is nearly twice as high as Sweden's. Ten thousand births a year take place without a doctor, and in the North American tradition there are no midwives. In some provinces the figures for child neglect are formidable. In Quebec there are orphanages for up to three thousand children under one roof; in one institution for infants an epidemic killed half the children. Rehabilitation services for the disabled and crippled are only just beginning. The national hospital insurance plan is still only a scheme for the future; there is as yet no agreement between the six provinces who have said they will participate. [As of April 1959, seven of the ten provinces had free or nearly free hospitalization plans designed to provide basic hospital care for Canadians regardless of income or financial resources. The exact working out of the plans varies from province to province. It should be noted that Canada's plan is principally a hospital insurance program and does not include medical care as in Great Britain.—Ed.]

In few places in Canada is there much feeling of civic responsibility. The poll in local elections is usually low; in many areas last autumn [1957] only 30 or 40 per cent. Men and women are reluctant to do much voluntary public work. Although the proportion of married women who do paid work is much smaller than in Britain, in 11 out of 43 cities no woman has ever sat either on the council or on the education or hospital boards.

Canada is rich in eminent and responsible sociologists, town planners, doctors, priests, teachers and industrialists who are well aware of the danger to human beings of some aspects of industrialism and who work hard for safeguards. Some examples of the most efficient social institutions in North America are to be found in Canada. But the social engineers will have to work as quickly as their industrial counterparts. If they do not hasten their task of altering public opinion, of pricking social consciences, then Canada will become a country of bleak contrasts between rich and poor, a country of great wealth existing within a vast area of poverty—of the mind as well as the purse.

FAMILY ALLOWANCES [9]

[Children under sixteen years of age who are resident in Canada are eligible for family allowances. The allowances, which were established in 1945, are paid from general revenue by the Department of National Health and Welfare, involve no means test and are not considered as income for tax purposes. Allowances are paid at the monthly rate of $6 for children under ten years and $8 for children ten to fifteen years of age.

Through the Department of Citizenship and Immigration the federal government also pays, on a monthly basis, an allowance of sixty dollars a year for each child under sixteen years of age supported by an immigrant who has landed for permanent residence in Canada or by a Canadian returning to Canada to reside permanently. This allowance is paid for a period of one year, until the child is eligible for family allowance.—Ed.]

Every study made in Canada has demonstrated that the bulk of family-allowance funds soon find their way into channels of trade and business. In 1951, after family allowances had been distributed for six years, researchers at Laval University in Quebec discovered that the allowances had been used most frequently for the following purposes:

1. Children's clothing
2. Insurance policies and annuities for children
3. Medical care and medicines for children
4. More nutritious food for children
5. Children's savings accounts in banks and other savings institutions
6. Toys and amusement for children

Family allowances require about 8 per cent of the total budget of the national government of Canada. This is a substantial proportion. It exceeds by 3 per cent the proportion of the U.S.

[9] From article by Senator Richard L. Neuberger (Democrat, Oregon). *America.* 97:189-91. May 11, 1957. Reprinted from *America* (America Press, New York 17, N.Y.)

budget that goes to all labor-and-welfare matters. It likewise exceeds by exactly 3 per cent the proportion of our Federal budget that a program of family allowances would constitute, should our Congress enact legislation patterned precisely after the Canadian plan. . . .

What do Canadians themselves think of the government checks which are mailed on the twentieth day of each month to mothers or principal guardians of Canadian boys and girls?

I was serving in the Yukon Territory with the American troops building the great Alcan Highway to Fairbanks when such men as the then Prime Minister Mackenzie King, Father Léon Lebel and Professor Leonard Marsh were discussing the idea of family allowances. Canadians confessed to me their skepticism. This was particularly true of families who felt they could raise their children "without a sop from Ottawa." A Gallup Poll in 1943 showed that slightly less than 50 per cent of Canadians favored the proposal. Many of the opponents were vocal and vehement.

Between the end of World War II in 1945 and my election to the U. S. Senate in 1954, my wife and I returned to Canada each year to gather material for books and articles. We talked with literally hundreds of Canadians—with Indians and Eskimos, Hudson's Bay Company factors, Catholic and Anglican missionaries, members of parliament, train conductors, mounted police officers, utility executives, fishermen, nurses, teachers. We saw opposition to family allowances slowly but steadily wane, even on the part of our most conservative Canadian friends.

A 1950 Gallup Poll showed 90 per cent of the people of Canada in favor of family allowances. There has been no serious criticism of the program in parliament for almost a decade. All the major political parties today accept the program as a worthwhile feature of the country's national life. . . .

During the first year that family allowances were in force, infant mortality in Canada dropped from 51 to 47 per 1,000 births—a most heartening and welcome development. In the same period, the monthly production of children's shoes soared from 762,000 pairs to 1.18 million pairs, a prodigious increase of over 54 per cent.

On the streets of Edmonton, Mrs. Neuberger and I have seen long lines of mothers and children waiting to purchase shoes a day or so after the monthly family-allowances check was due in each household. Traders at remote wilderness outposts told us there had been no real demand for Pablum or vitamins until family allowances went into effect. The number of Canadian doctors specializing in pediatrics has multiplied many times since the system was adopted.

At the British Columbia community of Revelstoke, in the heart of the towering Selkirk Mountains, I met a Canadian Pacific locomotive engineer. He and his attractive wife had five young children. Their first few family-allowances payments each year were used to finance a thorough medical and dental checkup at a local clinic for all five children. Several potentially serious difficulties had thus been detected in ample time.

Would the engineer and his wife have undertaken such an expenditure if they had received merely a tax reduction? Would the reduction have carried with it the compulsion to do something specifically for the children, as is the case with family allowances?

V. DIVERSITY AND UNITY

EDITOR'S INTRODUCTION

Canada, with its two official languages, its minority groups—Eskimos, Indians, Hindus, religious sects—and its economic cleavages, has always been culturally and socially diverse. Within the past decade—due to immigration and economic change—some new differences have appeared while at the same time social differentiation has been receding. Along with this a new interest has been developing among Canadians in what it means to be "Canadian." Is there emerging out of diversity some universal way of life which represents a Canadian culture?

In the first ten years after World War II almost one and a half million immigrants were admitted into Canada. These immigrants, according to the first article in this section, were predominantly male and most likely to be from the Commonwealth countries, though in 1957 many Hungarian refugees and Dutch farmers joined their ranks. In a second article Michael Barkway, a Canadian journalist, raises a basic question about future immigration policy: may the baby boom, by supplying the need for manpower, render the continued pace of immigration unnecessary? The Northwestern territories, as pointed out in the following selection, have wooed and welcomed immigrants. Once settled, the newcomers in general enjoy a higher standard of living than in their country of origin. A fourth article describes the social and cultural change which European immigrants (many of them Catholic) have brought about in Toronto, stronghold of British Protestant Canada.

The next group of articles highlight some of the problems of social diversity. Dennis Wrong maintains that the "melting-pot" concept has not come to the Canadian scene. There is a social distance between those of British origin and other Canadians of whatever origin so that social discrimination persists. An article in the *U.S. News & World Report* shows how the

French-English split has led to the maintenance of two separate public school systems. Religious segregation has official sanction: it both reflects the schism and reenforces it. The seventh article points to a basic difference in two official approaches to the Eskimo problem: one wants to preserve the traditional Eskimo culture, the other to integrate the Eskimo with the Canadian. As industry moves north, according to the writer, the chances are that the Eskimo will be integrated.

The last articles, reflecting the growth of Canadian nationalism, concern the need for or reality of a separate Canadian culture. Otto Butz's article focuses on the lack of a "past" which has made Canadian culture so vulnerable. He finds few positive assets apt to create a separate Canadian culture and criticizes the efforts of intellectuals, carried out "in a vacuum," to create one. In the next article Marshall MacLuhan, on the other hand, sees this lack of binding tradition as an asset. According to him Canada is free to pioneer in the new mass media (such as television) and to discard the Victorian tradition. The last two selections summarize some Canadian efforts to unify the country by building a Canadian tradition. Canadians are subsidizing television in an effort to weld the nation together much as railroads were once used to bind the confederation of provinces. The Arts Council (as well as the National Film Board and the Canadian Broadcasting Corporation) are subsidizing and encouraging Canadian talent. They look upon its promotion as one of their major responsibilities for the achievement of unity.

MAGNET FOR IMMIGRATION [1]

The United States has received more immigrants since World War II than any other country in the world. Between the years ended June 30, 1946 and 1957, over 2.6 million immigrants were admitted for permanent residence.

Canada, in like manner, has experienced a large immigration since World War II. In eight out of the eleven years 1946-1956

[1] From "United States and Canada: Magnets for Immigration," article by Helen F. Eckerson, chief, Statistics Branch, Immigration and Naturalization Service, United States Department of Justice. *Annals of the American Academy of Political and Social Sciences.* 316:34-43. March 1958. Reprinted by permission.

she was the second largest immigrant-receiving country; the total admitted through 1956 was 1,387,176, and by now it is well over 1.5 million. The impact of this immigration on a population of approximately 15 million is tremendous. It has added a population greater than that of British Columbia to the Canadian economy.

In the exchange of nationals between United States and Canada, 78,000 citizens born in the United States exchanged places with 293,000 citizens of Canada. . . .

For the years 1946-1955 immigration from Canada averaged about 23,000, but in 1956 was 29,000, and in 1957, 33,000. The attraction of the United States appears to be the opportunities for professional and technical advancement. In 1957 half of the 46,000 immigrants whose country of last residence was Canada were in the labor force, and of that number almost 6,000 were engineers, draftsmen, doctors, nurses, and teachers, and other professional and technical workers. Twenty-eight per cent of these immigrants were of European birth. . . .

Under the Canadian government's Assisted Passage Loan Scheme, put into effect in 1951, 32,054 persons obtained money to pay costs of their travel from Europe to their destination in Canada and agreed to repay the loans advanced within twenty-four months. The Scheme, begun for single persons and heads of families, was extended in 1955 to wives and children of the working head of the family. Of the more than 5 million dollars loaned by December 31, 1955, all but 6 per cent had been repaid.

The federal government has made agreements with most of the provinces to share equally the cost of welfare assistance and hospitalization for immigrants rendered indigent through accident or illness during the first year after their arrival in Canada.

Canada wants immigrants from Commonwealth countries, France, and the United States. Of the total 1,387,176 admitted during 1946-1956, there were 405,304, or 29 per cent, born in Commonwealth countries; 27,499, or 2 per cent, born in France; and 78,755, or 6 per cent, from the United States. The principal country of emigration was England with admissions of 260,786. In 1946 immigration from England was 38,991 when wives of Canadian servicemen were coming to Canada. It gradually decreased to a low of 8,419 in 1950 due to the devaluation of the pound sterling and lack of shipping. It has since increased gradually to over 31,000 in 1956.

While the United States has been receiving many professional and technical workers from Canada, the migration is not just a one-way operation. Nineteen per cent of the immigrations from the United States to Canada are in the professional group. Other sizable numbers are in the skilled trades. Almost a fourth of the immigrants from the United States were born in a country other than the United States.

In general, immigrants from other than the favored areas must either be sponsored by a Canadian resident relative or come for placement or to establish themselves in business. Approximately 30 to 40 per cent of immigrants are sponsored, the remainder are open-placement cases. That is, the needs of the Canadian economy are appraised and then the immigration officers are instructed as to what kinds of workers to admit.

Recruited workers are usually brought to Canada in the spring and summer, peak seasons for employment. Dependent wives and children follow in the fall and winter. Approximately 800 thousand such persons arrived, chiefly from the countries of Europe other than the United Kingdom and France, in the eleven years 1946-1956.

Canada, like the United States, supported the international measures to resettle postwar refugees and displaced persons. From 1948 to 1953 a total of 165,697 displaced persons were admitted, not including 3,235 Polish ex-servicemen admitted in 1946-1947 and granted permanent status in 1948. After the International Refugee Organization ceased its operations, provisions were continued for the admission of bona fide refugees, but no separate statistics are kept with respect to them.

Sixty-one per cent of the displaced persons were in the labor force. Most of them came to accept employment through group movements and in accordance with the occupations recommended by the Immigration-Labor Committee. The principal categories were farmers, unskilled and skilled workers (usually in the construction trades), and domestics.

The Hungarian revolution found Canada again in the forefront with a generous policy of admissions. As of September 30, 1957, 35,717 Hungarian refugees had been received. About 24,000 came to Canada under the International Committee for European Migration.

The movement of Netherlanders to Canada was begun in April 1947 and was carried out in close cooperation with the Netherlands government under whose auspices most of the farm families came. The Settlement Service within the Immigration Branch was responsible for overseeing settlement in Canada. Under the plan Canadian farmers undertook to provide employment and living accommodations for these immigrants for at least a year. A number of these Netherlands families have already purchased their own farms in Canada. In the years 1946 through 1956, a total of 115,417 immigrants born in the Netherlands entered Canada. . . .

Whereas immigrants admitted to the United States were predominantly females, those going to Canada were predominantly males. In 1946, when wives of Canadian servicemen were entering Canada, there were 4 males admitted to every 10 females. In 1947, the sex ratio shifted, fluctuating since then from an equal proportion to a high of 22 males per 10 females in 1954. In 1956 the ratio was 12 males to each 10 female immigrants admitted. . . . The median age of immigrants admitted to Canada in 1956 was 24.9 for males and 25.0 for females.

Fifty-five per cent of the immigrants were in the labor force, with 7 per cent in the professional group and 30 per cent in the mechanical and construction group. The large majority were skilled construction workers; 12 per cent were in service occupations, including 66,150 domestic servants. The other principal groups were laborers and clerical workers.

As in the United States, the heavily populated provinces were the ones that received the most immigrants. Over half of the immigrants admitted in 1946-1956 were going to Ontario, 20 per cent to Quebec, 9 per cent to British Columbia, 8 per cent to Alberta, and 5 per cent to Manitoba.

TURNING POINT FOR IMMIGRATION? [2]

Canada's postwar immigration policy passed its tenth anniversary on May 1, 1957, without mourners or celebrants. It had its origins in a statement made to the House of Commons on May 1, 1947, by Mr. Mackenzie King. Since then, the Department of Citizenship and Immigration has been established, the Immigration Act has been revised, and the Regulations have been rewritten. The broad outline of Mr. King's statement has been developed into a more mature and expressive picture. But all this has developed Mr. King's policy rather than altering it. There is still no better source for an explanation of Canada's immigration policy than Mr. King's 1947 statement. . . .

Mr. King's statement on May 1, 1947, was characteristic of him and of the period. It laid down smooth-sounding principles of delightful rotundity, and gave hardly any indication how they were to be applied. After dealing with the immediate problem of rescuing displaced persons and others from the emergency camps of an overcrowded postwar Europe, Mr. King came to the long-term policy, and said:

The government's long-term program is based on the conviction that Canada needs population . . .
The government is strongly of the view that our immigration policy should be devised in a positive sense, with the definitive objective, as I have already stated, of enlarging the population of the country . . .
The fear has been expressed that immigration would lead to a reduction in the standard of living. This need not be the case. If immigration is properly planned, the result will be the reverse. A larger population will help to develop our resources. By providing a larger number of consumers, in other words a larger domestic market, it will reduce the present dependence of Canada on the export of primary products.
The essential thing is that immigrants be selected with care, and that their numbers be adjusted to the absorptive capacity of the country.
It is of the utmost importance to relate immigration to absorptive capacity. . . .
The object of the government is to secure what new population we can absorb, but not to exceed that number. The figure that represents our absorptive capacity will clearly vary from year to year in response to

[2] From pamphlet by Michael Barkway, Ottowa correspondent for the *Financial Post*. (Behind the Headlines. vol 17, no 4) Canadian Institute of International Affairs. Toronto, Ontario. 1957. p4-9, 15-16. Reprinted by permission.

economic conditions. . . . At the present stage it is impossible with any degree of accuracy to make forecasts as to our future power of absorption. . . .

When [shipping ceases to be a limitation] . . ., it will be necessary to consider further what measures will best achieve the adjustment of immigration to the numbers that can be absorbed into the economy of Canada.

So much for the numerical yardstick. What kind of people did Mr. King favor? [He said]

I wish to make it quite clear that Canada is perfectly within her rights in selecting the persons whom we regard as desirable future citizens. It is not a "fundamental human right" of an alien to enter Canada. It is a privilege. It is a matter of domestic policy. . . .

He then announced repeal of the Chinese Immigration Act, so that Chinese residents of Canada might become Canadian citizens, and thereafter be allowed to bring in their wives and unmarried children under eighteen. The Indians as Canadian citizens would have the same right. But Japanese would not be admitted to Canada. Mr. King went on:—

There will, I am sure, be general agreement with the view that the people of Canada do not wish, as a result of mass immigration, to make a fundamental change in the character of our population.

Large-scale immigration from the Orient would change the fundamental composition of the Canadian population. . . . The Government has no thought of making any change in immigration regulations which would have consequences of that kind. . . .

Canada recognizes the right of all other countries to control the entry or non-entry of persons seeking to become permanent residents. We claim precisely the same right for our country. . . .

[The order of precedence as it has since been officially designated is as follows.—Ed.]

1. Europeans from: Austria, Belgium, Denmark, West Germany, Finland, Greece, Iceland, Italy, Luxembourg, the Netherlands, Norway, Portugal, Spain, Sweden, Switzerland. Also refugees. On condition:

"If such person undertakes to come to Canada for placement under the auspices of the Department, or, if the Department has given its approval thereto, for establishment in a business, trade or profession or in agriculture."

2. Israel, Egypt, Lebanon, Turkey; any other European country; any country of North, Central or South America (meant to include the West Indian islands). On condition that they are "close relatives" of Canadian residents able to look after them, "close relatives" being defined in comparatively broad terms.

3. From anywhere else, only "close relatives" defined in very narrow terms.

4. From India, Pakistan and Ceylon in accordance with special agreements providing for the admission each year of 150, 100 and 50 people respectively.

5. From Trinidad and Jamaica, special arrangements permitting very limited admission for stated numbers of domestics and nurses.

Mr. King insisted that the number of immigrants to be admitted each year must be fitted to the "absorptive capacity" of the economy. This remains the essential yardstick. But it is not easy to apply. It must involve some crystal-gazing, and the seer's task is doubly difficult when every immigrant is expected to find a job as soon as he lands.

This is how the administration works.

At intervals during the year the Immigration Department and the Labor Department try to agree how many immigrants can be "readily placed in employment" (Mr. King's phrase) in the coming summer or winter, and what occupations will have the best chance.

Since the average time between an immigrant's final acceptance and his arrival in Canada is about six months, summer prospects need to be calculated well before the end of the preceding year. The fall-winter outlook should be settled in the spring.

Naturally the Labor officials' main concern is to avoid unemployment. The Immigration officials are more concerned with Mr. King's idea of a "positive" policy for increasing the population of Canada and the size of the domestic market. . . .

Detailed estimates of job openings form the bible of the immigration officers overseas. From these lists they decide whether to admit each applicant (In the United Kingdom or France, merely what advice to give); and they can advise each successful applicant where his best chances lie in Canada. Once the immigrant arrives, however, he can go where he likes. No one will direct him where to go or what job to take, except perhaps in extreme cases where he shows an inclination to go on living on the government.

That's a rough outline of present methods. It would be unfair to say they have served us badly. But they have been applied through a period when Canada's need for extra workers was extremely pressing. How well will they serve if that need loses its urgency?

The new problem for 1958 and later years arises from the drastic change in the pattern of population growth. . . . The increase in births from the low level of the 'thirties started in 1940 and has continued even more sharply ever since. We began to feel the effect in 1955, but mildly. It is growing each year. The schools are feeling it; the universities are preparing for it. Fewer people seem to have thought about its effects on the employment picture. But nearly half the boys between 14 and 19 go to work and about one-third of the girls.

Elaborate projections of the labor force aren't necessary. We know that death rates are falling; and we can count at each census the children growing up. They are already with us. Their impact on the labor force may be delayed a little if they stay longer at school, but a rate of increase far beyond what we have known is inescapable.

This means, simply, that we have had a ten-year reprieve before having to decide how far we really believe Mr. King's proposition. He said: "A larger population will help to develop our resources. By providing a larger number of consumers, in other words a larger domestic market, it will reduce the present dependence of Canada on the export of primary products."

The words have a strangely topical note now. After ten years' growth Canada is more, not less, dependent on the export of primary materials, largely in unprocessed form, largely from companies under United States control. Although the domestic market is now a third larger than it was in 1947, secondary manufacturing holds a relatively lower position in the economy.

Do Canadians still believe in giving the expansion of the domestic market an extra boost by immigration? If they do, new methods will have to be devised to meet the new situation. For soon we shall have an increasing number of consumers and workers even without importing any. . . .

Conclusion

A policy blueprint for the future, suited to the new conditions when immigrants, instead of marching into an aching void in the working population, may have to be fitted in with a shoehorn, obviously cannot be attempted within the bounds of this pamphlet. It will in any case require the brains of the best economists and the most experienced social workers to work it out. But the task won't be started until the problem is much more widely accepted.

Here I have only tried to indicate three of its obvious difficulties:

1. From now on, with Canadian youngsters filling the labor force vacancies which immigrants have been taking since the war, new methods of settlement may be necessary. If immigration is to be maintained at all, it may well be impossible to go on throwing the newcomers indiscriminately onto the labor market as soon as they arrive.

2. With seasonal unemployment unhappily increasing in amplitude, it grows increasingly unsatisfactory to admit everyone we may hope to employ in summer, and then to stop the flow as soon as we are hit by the annual scare about winter unemployment.

3. In the new circumstances it will be necessary to make much more purposeful arrangements for helping immigrants to adapt to Canadian ways and fitting them into a useful place in Canadian life.

IMMIGRANTS AND THE NORTH [3]

Trees looked like shrubs in the spacious countryside; the small houses were set at wide intervals along the lake. The

[3] From "Bird's Eye View of Canada: Where Malthus Is No Prophet," article by special correspondent. *Economist.* 181:1135-6. December 29, 1956. Reprinted by permission.

Hudson's Bay Company's store was stocked, necessarily, to supply all wants. Yellowknife is a man's town, built on gold. The nearest big shopping center, Edmonton, lies 700 miles to the south.

To a tourist on a fleeting visit this solitude has a romantic appeal. People compelled to live there all the year round feel differently; so do the mining companies, faced with the difficulty of getting manpower. Higher wages and the refunding of fares after a certain period of work are two methods used to keep this multilingual labor force fairly stable. People go so far north to get money quickly. Some actually do go south again after a year or two with substantial savings; others cannot stand the loneliness for long; still others drown it in whisky.

Yellowknife presents in a nutshell the problem of the unconquered North, a question of distances even more than of climate. The Northwestern Territories of Canada, lying above the sixtieth parallel, cover an area of about 1.3 million square miles, equivalent to one-third of continental Europe, but Yellowknife, with its 3,000 inhabitants, accounts for nearly one-fifth of the total population. A few thousand Eskimos, dependent on the vagaries of the fur trade; a few thousand Indians, fitting uneasily into the new pattern of life; and less than 6,000 white people in key positions—these are the only inhabitants of this vast area. It is potentially one of the richest in the world. Furs and gold are no longer the only lure. Pitchblende extracted at Port Radium includes radium salts, uranium and cobalt, while the whole territory is apparently a geologist's paradise. But a major shift of population northwards lies in the future. In the meantime, each new strike by the pioneering explorers will help the growth of the secondary industries in the more hospitable and populated South.

Canadians lag far behind the Russians in developing their "Siberia." Hitherto neither shortage of materials nor pressure of population have been a sufficient incentive. Indeed, Canada has to look for foreign labor to maintain its pace of expansion. Immigration is no longer controlled by the land available. The bulk of newcomers are entering other branches of the economy. Though the birth-rate has risen appreciably from the depressed level of the thirties—it averaged about 2 per cent in the last five years—the Canadian government seems sufficiently confident in the future to continue encouraging immigration on a large scale. During the postwar decade the population of Canada was swollen by 1.2 million newcomers, of whom more than half were men of working age.

No random sample can give an accurate picture of the life of these new Canadians. Reactions vary from place to place and from person to person. Two young Londoners who reached Vancouver at the time of a seasonal recession described the rough time they had to begin with. Several professional people also complained that the first steps were difficult. It seems generally agreed, however, that once settled the newcomers enjoy a higher standard of life than they had in their country of origin.

To say that the average weekly wage in Canada last year was over £20 [$56] means little, because exchange rates are deceptive. Migrants, who stick to a similar job, however, confirm that their real wages are much higher. A patternmaker—admittedly a skilled workman—who had moved from an English foundry to Edmonton may serve as an illustration. We drove to his spotless bungalow in a big American car. The drawing room was dominated by a giant television screen. In the kitchen stood a man-size refrigerator (he was still just below the "deep freeze class"), a washing machine, a special ironing device and all sorts of other gadgets. He thought it would have taken a lifetime back home to acquire everything that he had collected here in a few years. He, for one, was glad of the change and spoke nostalgically only of his *Daily Mirror* and the League soccer game on Saturday.

More sophisticated expatriates from London risk finding Canada's cultural life somewhat provincial. This may be the price of its industrial revolution. Fast growing countries tend to have little time for cultural luxuries. But by now wealthy Canada should be able to develop its own distinctive voice from out of its mixed heritage. Some people wonder whether the American-inspired passion for more and different gadgets is not hindering such a development.

People do not, however, emigrate in search of culture. They leave Europe in order to seek better living conditions overseas. As long as its extraordinary postwar boom lasts, Canada, with its higher wages, lower taxes and greater opportunities, will attract men, particularly young men, from Britain and the European continent. Each time clouds gather on the economic or the political horizon in Europe this flow of migrants will quicken, as it is doing now.

NEWCOMERS AND THE CITIES [4]

An explosive burst of immigration is changing the face of the Catholic Church in Canada. It is changing Canada. Beginning with the end of World War II, it reached a climax in 1956-1957 with the arrival of more Hungarian refugees than were received by any other country. Though the flow has lessened, it continues at a steady rate.

It has affected the Archdiocese of Toronto, the industrial heartland of the country, more than any other region. What was, so recently as a decade ago, an American-oriented but sentimentally British, English-speaking and fundamentally Protestant provincial city, has become a roaring metropolis where any day in the subway the visitor unaware of what has happened will be startled by the Babel of tongues.

No city in the world has grown more strikingly than Toronto in these last ten years. The skyline changes with the weeks; suburbs have proliferated like a thousand Levittowns. Catholics were in a small minority a few years ago, but parishes and separate schools (i.e., public though separate) have been established at the rate of about one every couple of months. There are today thirty parishes that did not exist five years ago.

Where a decade ago the Archbishop, James Cardinal Mc-Guigan, alone carried the episcopal duties of the archdiocese, he now has two auxiliary bishops; and one Ukrainian Catholic bishop has his see in Toronto. To the metropolitan area have

[4] From article entitled "Canadian Church in Flux" by J. E. Belliveau, a columnist for the Toronto *Daily Star*. *America*. 99:349-50. June 21, 1958. Reprinted from *America* (America Press, New York 17, N.Y.)

come 75,000 Italians, 30,000 Hungarians, 70,000 Germans, many of them Catholics; and Poles, Czechs, Yugoslavs, Maltese, Spaniards, French, Belgians, Dutch, Bulgarians, Rumanians, Lebanese, Austrians, Irish and many others in smaller groups. Of the 300,000 Catholics in the city area, a full 150,000 are Europeans come within the last decade.

As a Catholic archdiocese, Toronto is still, of course, smaller than Montreal. That vastly expanding metropolis is 70 per cent French and at least 80 per cent Catholic. Toronto, however, is more cosmopolitan now, though Montreal, as the nation's largest city, has also been a haven for European immigrants.

It might have been expected that Montreal, with its French, Catholic and Europeanized culture, would have attracted the newcomers in greater numbers, but this has not been the case. They came instead to a city that is traditionally staid and more British than the Britons. Toronto isn't that any more. The immigrants came to a city that was the Protestant, and militantly Protestant, capital of Canada; and perhaps the happiest thing of all has been the peaceful nature of the evolution they brought about there.

Among the factors that few even in Toronto appreciate is that the total immigration to Toronto has been as much Canadian as European. It has brought to the city tens of thousands of French Canadians, Catholics to a man. Not all are from French Quebec. Many are from the provinces of New Brunswick, Nova Scotia and Prince Edward Island, where the French Acadians are descendants of the first European settlers in all America north of St. Augustine, Florida.

Where the modern Canadian mass immigration has differed from that of another generation in the United States is in the higher educational standards of those who have come. A peasant and working-class influx filled the American cities, but a majority perhaps of those who have come recently to Canada, to the towns and farms as well as to the cities, belonged to the middle class or to commercial, professional and academic groups.

Mostly, of course, they were political refugees; and they brought with them not only their academic achievements, their abilities and their brains, but also their ethical attitudes. They are majestically anti-Communist; they are politically alert, and their leaders have moved swiftly into the field of politics.

The new Canadians have been assiduously courted by the political parties, and party leaders have been on their mettle to keep abreast of events and ideas chronicled in the massively spreading ethnic press. In Toronto, in the March 31 [1958] election for the Federal Parliament, Dr. John Kucherepa, a Ukrainian and a former city alderman, was reelected as a Conservative M.P. Dr. Stanley Haidasz, a Polish scholar and a Liberal, lost his seat in the Conservative alndslide. And a man with the unlikely name, for a Canadian, of Jack Kedzierzykowski ran (unsuccessfully) for Parliament on the mildly Socialist Commonwealth Cooperative Federation ticket in a third Toronto constituency. . . .

In earlier migrations, it was the custom of lower-income people to settle and remain in enclaves of their own. This is not today's condition. Many of the European arrivals are people of means, and others achieve wealth quickly—like the Toronto Slovak who in less than a decade has become a financial mining magnate worth millions.

Many, even in the beginning, go to the middle-class suburbs to live. . . .

Perhaps the most cheering side of the immigration picture is the tolerance with which the newcomers have been accepted. What has happened in Toronto has happened elsewhere to a smaller degree. As the Europeans entered the arts of music, painting and architecture, and into the professions and the scholarly world, they found a speedy acceptance.

Because so many moved in scholarly, artistic and intellectual circles, they did not meet with the resentments, the narrowness, the bigotry of an earlier time. They have, for instance, made a secure place for themselves in television, where their production ability and artistic talents were needed by a country that has been busier about making a living than about developing the arts. The architecture of our new churches, often ultramodern in spirit and décor, has shown the influence of the immigrants.

Fortunately, too, most of the immigrants came in a time of expanding economy, so that even now, with unemployment a problem, they have not been accused of displacing native Canadians from jobs to the degree that they would have been in other times.

What has happened in Toronto may be a mirror for the future in Canada. This bustling, modern, ebullient land of vast expanses has needed just this cultural shot in the arm. And the immigrants have needed the optimistic, expansive and forward-looking openness that has characterized Canada in her period of greatest development. It has been a happy union.

SOCIAL DISCRIMINATION [5]

The absence of a fully developed sense of Canadian nationality has retarded the application of the melting-pot concept to the Canadian scene. As A. R. M. Lower has noted,

"New Canadians" in Canada have had little chance of becoming "Canadians" in the same sense that they would become American in the United States. In that country distinctions of origin are, in theory at least, kept to a minimum; in Canada they are practically and in certain ways legally maintained.

In public discussions of New Canadians the emphasis tends to be on the contributions which the diverse cultural heritages they bring with them will make to Canadian life rather than, as is commonly the case in the United States, on their expectations of life in the New World. New Canadians have been encouraged to maintain many of their distinctive folk traditions, and their songs, dress, and folklore are often publicized as indications of the richness and diversity of Canadian life—an approach to ethnic differences that is much less common in the United States where retaining Old World habits has often been stigmatized as refusal to become good Americans or to appreciate adequately the superiority of the "American way of life."

[5] From *American and Canadian Viewpoints,* pamphlet by Dennis Wrong, Canadian sociologist. American Council on Education. Washington, D.C. 1955. p49-51. Reprinted by permission.

Other reasons in addition to the lack of a clear-cut Canadian nationality explain the greater acceptance in Canada of a "cultural pluralist" approach to ethnic minority groups: Canada is a binational state uniting two culturally divergent peoples under a single system of government, a circumstance which obviously makes it impossible to advance a single uniform conception of the "Canadian way of life" for immigrants to emulate; also, in western Canada some ethnic communities have remained geographically and sometimes occupationally segregated from the native-born population, reproducing in this respect the pattern of settlement and of consequent ethnic particularism of many of the major groups making up the "old immigration" to the United States before the First World War.

In addition to appreciation of cultural diversity, however, there also appears to be a marked sense of social distance between those of British origin and the foreign-born or even second- and third-generation immigrants. Many forms of social discrimination have persisted in Canada which in the United States, although they survive there too, have increasingly been condemned as undemocratic. In the United States highly vocal campaigns against prejudice and discrimination have tended to drive expressions of prejudice underground or into extreme "lunatic fringe" forms of political protest, whereas in Canada genteel expressions of prejudice and the practice of social discrimination appear to be more widely accepted as a matter of course, at least tacitly if not openly. A good many observers, for example, have reported their impression that anti-Semitism is both more widespread and more open in Canadian than in American life. Yet, as in the United States, even the mildest forms of prejudice have increasingly come under attack. In political campaigns in both countries (with the exception of the American South) a covert appeal to prejudice is likely to bring down such a storm of criticism on the head of the candidate who makes it that he risks losing more votes than he might gain from the support of the prejudiced.

French-speaking Canadians are not a minority group in the sense that recent overseas immigrants are in view of the constitutional guarantees maintaining the use of their language and the practice of their religion, but statistically they are an ethnic and religious minority in the population of Canada. There is a sense in which French Canadians may be described as more successful practitioners of cultural pluralism than any of the other ethnic groups in North America who, when in the minority have usually experienced considerable tension between their ethnic and national loyalties, and, when in the majority have practiced discrimination against those who differed from themselves in ethnic origin. The French Canadians' desire to preserve their language, religion, and traditional customs has only rarely conflicted with their allegiance to the Canadian nation. Ethnic loyalty to their group and political allegiance to Canada have existed side by side. While they have occasionally been at odds in the past over such issues as the Manitoba schools question and military conscription in the two world wars, their continued coexistence is becoming more and more natural to French Canadians with the decline of separatist sentiment in recent years.

In their attitude to immigrant groups from overseas, French Canadians have not been particularly receptive to the possibility of assimilating them into French-Canadian culture. Most non-English speaking immigrants to Canada have settled in areas where English is the main language and have absorbed the culture of English-speaking rather than of French-speaking Canada. This has usually been true even of Catholic immigrants. There is some evidence that Italians settling in Montreal have learned French as their second language, but very little information is available concerning the extent to which immigrants settling in predominantly French-Canadian towns and cities have tended to assimilate into the French-Canadian culture, or of the attitudes toward them of the French Canadians. In Montreal there has been conflict and antagonism between French Canadians and Jews in areas where the two groups have been economic competitors, and anti-Semitism has been common throughout French Canada. On the whole, however, the French Canadian has adopted a "live and let live" attitude toward minority ethnic groups in Canada as long as the newcomers have not interfered with or challenged the French-Canadian way of life.

SCHOOLS: PUBLIC BUT SEPARATE [6]

A system of segregated, or separate, schools is being supported in Canada with public funds. In this system, schools are voluntarily separated on the basis of religion. . . . Regulation of public education is left completely to each province and local community, all ten provinces . . . [permitting] public assistance in some form to schools organized on the basis of religious faith.

An example of how the Canadian system works can be found in Ontario. Here, in a population of 5.4 million, there is a strong minority of Roman Catholics, most of whom live in the eastern section adjacent to the Province of Quebec, largely populated by Catholics of French descent.

Taxpayers in Ontario support either "public" schools or "separate" schools up through the elementary grades. There are no separate high schools. Those elementary schools designed as "separate" actually are, for the most part, Catholic schools.

In most sections of Ontario, Catholics, in a minority, are given the privilege of allocating their school taxes for the support of these separate schools. Protestants, making up the majority, do not have the same choice. Their taxes go to support the public schools. . . .

In the case of mixed marriages, it is the wish of the father, as legal "head of the house," that governs the allocation of taxes. If the father is a Catholic and has a Protestant wife, he has the choice of supporting either public or separate schools. If he is a Protestant with a Catholic wife, his taxes go to support the public schools, even though his wife may want to send her children to Catholic schools.

Catholics in Ontario also are given the right to change their school support at any time. Some send their children to public schools for the first few years and then switch them to separate Catholic schools. Parents are permitted to change their support from one school system to the other whenever they choose to do so. . . .

[6] From article entitled "Where Public Funds Support 'Separate' Schools." *U.S. News & World Report.* 43:109-10. December 20, 1957. Reprinted from *U.S. News & World Report,* an independent weekly news magazine published at Washington, D.C. Copyright 1957 United States News Publishing Corporation.

If there are no separate schools in an area where there is a Catholic or Protestant minority, such groups may, under the Ontario law, require one to be established by local authorities. Five or more "heads of families" may join together, elect their own school board and set up their own religious school. The school then is eligible for public support. At any time, however, the minority taxpayers have the option either of supporting this school with their taxes or using their tax funds to support the public schools.

Separate schools in Ontario are under the control of local boards of education. In the city of Ottawa, which has 40 public elementary schools and 35 separate elementary schools, there are two school boards, one Catholic and one Protestant. Each is elected by the voters registered on the basis of their religious faiths. Each board is under control of the provincial department of education at Toronto, and each must conform to the department's curriculum and other standards.

Among Canada's provinces, Ontario gives most freedom of choice to religious minorities in their use of the public schools. Other Canadian provinces, however, practice voluntary segregation on the religious level.

Quebec, overwhelmingly Roman Catholic, goes even further in separation than any other province. This province separates its schools on a religious basis from kindergarten to university level. Each taxpayer pays taxes to support the schools which represent his religious beliefs. Taxes collected from corporations are divided between Catholic and non-Catholic schools on a per-pupil basis. Minorities in Quebec, moreover, cannot change their support from one school system to the other.

Nova Scotia, Prince Edward Island, New Brunswick, Manitoba and British Columbia extend privileges to religious minorities in the schools, either by law or by general agreement. Many local communities in Nova Scotia, New Brunswick and Prince Edward Island provide for voluntary segregation on the basis of religion. Manitoba permits religious instruction for minorities in the public schools. In British Columbia, free textbooks are furnished to students attending private or parochial schools.

Alberta and Saskatchewan permit separate school boards to conduct schools for religious minorities.

Almost everywhere in Canada, in other words, religious segregation in the public schools has official sanction.

THE PLASTIC IGLOO [7]

Canadians are inclined to be fonder of their Eskimo population than of their Indian. The two groups have the same Mongol origins and probably reached Canada at about the same time as part of the legendary migration across the frozen Bering Straits from Siberia. But about two thousand years ago the Eskimos moved north away from the other Indians, and while many of the original groups merged, the Canadian Eskimos beyond the tree line kept their way of life distinct. The coming of the white man did not concern them, while to the pioneers they remained a curiosity, remote and self-contained, in no way menacing white domination of North America. Perhaps this is why they are preferred. Their habits are not immediately prepossessing (though dictated by necessity): the Eskimos do not wash much and, as their name is believed to signify, sometimes eat their meat and fish raw. But while the Indians threatened the survival of the pioneers, the Eskimos were safely hidden away in land which, it was believed, no sane European would covet.

Now that the Canadians have begun to covet their North, both for defense and for economic reasons, the problem is what to do with the Eskimo. Until a few years ago it looked as if this was solving itself in the simplest and most brutal way. By 1951 less than ten thousand had survived the measles, tuberculosis and soap brought north by traders, missionaries and mounted police—perhaps a quarter of the Canadian Eskimo population a hundred years ago. Immunity from measles gradually acquired, and the setting up of excellent medical services, have stopped the decline (although even now one out of every twelve Eskimos is in hospital with tuberculosis). But it is no longer possible for all of them to keep themselves alive by the traditional skills of

[7] Reprint of article by special correspondent. *Economist.* 184:390-1. August 3, 1957. Reprinted by permission.

hunting and trapping. Firearms and synthetics are putting an end to this way of life. With guns in their hands, the Eskimo hunters are often wasteful and indiscriminate in their slaughter of caribou, their main source of food and clothing. They kill more animals than can be carried away at once and often the extra carcasses are buried by snowfall or eaten by wolves. In the last five years the game supply has been cut by more than half. The fur market has not been able to stand up against synthetics: even some of the Eskimos themselves wear nylon fur. White fox has become far too precarious a source of cash income, and officials in the Northern Affairs Department (which is responsible for Eskimo welfare) are aware that they have not only got to stop the Eskimos dying, but also to find some means of keeping them alive.

There are basically two ways of approaching the Eskimo problem, and the department has not quite made up its mind between the two. The one attitude respects deeply the traditional Eskimo characteristics and tries to preserve them; the other attempts to integrate the Eskimo population with the white Canadian. The danger of the first solution is that it can become as artificial as the plastic igloo which one official advocates; the snag to the second is that it may not work. More than half the Eskimos are still somehow living by hunting and fishing hundreds of miles from any white man; the ones who come to the settlements are inclined to be shy and bad mixers. There is a danger that without help and protection the isolated Eskimo may not survive, while the others might just become hewers of wood for the white men. But the supporters of a policy of natural integration have a powerful weapon in the example of the Indian reserves.

The policy of keeping the Indians isolated in reserves is now generally acknowledged to have been a failure. The artificiality of the thinly subsidized reserves has had disastrous effects on Indian morale and self-respect. Outside the reserves the Indian Canadian is a perfectly ordinary worker and citizen: inside, voteless, often jobless and irresponsible, he may sell the floor boards of his shack for a drink. The Indian reserves are not pleasant places; there is no reason to believe that an Eskimo community artificially kept alive would fare better.

Like the Eskimo who compromises in his dress, the Department of Northern Affairs steers a rather undecided course between tradition and change. The Eskimos who still live by hunting and fishing are helped, but only a little, in the hope that they will not come to rely on outside assistance. They are provided with hunting equipment if a bad season leaves them with no money; occasionally a group of them is moved to an area where it is known that they will intercept a herd of caribou; two months ago a big community in some distress was flown 150 miles north to join up with other groups on Resolute Bay. Attempts to make the Eskimos adopt less wasteful hunting methods seldom have much success. New ways of making money in winter are thought up and fostered, the most important being the revival of Eskimo carving. These stumpy little sculptures of men and beasts made from walrus tusks or sandstone are in the direct tradition of ancient carvings, and the simplicity and humor with which they are done has made them popular. Other prospects for winter industry include boat building and the collection of eider duck feathers. Actual distress is staved off by these devices, but the central problems—the decline of the game supply and the poor fur market—are untouched.

Where the Eskimos have joined with white communities, either in the construction of the Distant Early Warning Line which girdles Canada's Arctic, at other defense works or in northern mining towns, the problems are sorting themselves out rather satisfactorily. The Eskimos have proved to be such excellent electricians, plumbers and tinsmiths—picking up a skilled trade in half the time of most white men—that there is no question of using them only on unskilled labor. Their minds are unusually receptive, and once they have accepted the idea of staying in one place to work they are good and reliable employees. The older people hardly mix with other races, but a few of the children go to mixed schools. The northern affairs department provides good houses—excellent in comparison with the Indian shacks—and wages in the North are high. When the construction of the DEW Line is completed, it is unlikely that the Eskimo workers there will want to return to bad hunting for unwanted furs. They are far more likely to migrate to the new mines, where they are needed and where they will earn good money. As industry moves north into Canada's Arctic, the theory of the plastic igloo becomes exceedingly unrealistic.

CAN CANADIAN CULTURE SURVIVE? [8]

What is the nature of this threat to Canadian culture as Canadians see it? It is, in brief, this. Incessantly and with steadily increasing intensity, Canada is being subjected to an American cultural invasion in the form of books, magazines, broadcasts, lectures, artistic performances, scholarships and every other type of modern cultural commodity. This invasion, in which, it is admitted, the vast majority of Canadians seems only too happy to acquiesce, is rapidly transforming the country's social, ideological and psychological make-up into a national cultural complexion which with each passing year is becoming less distinguishable from that found south of the border.

Specifically, for example, some two-thirds of the books read by Canadians are printed in the United States (and the percentage for English-speaking Canada is considerably higher still). The best selling magazines in Canada are the same as those which have the greatest appeal among the American public—*Life, Time, The Reader's Digest*. . . . In the words of the Royal Commission,

Canadian magazines with much difficulty have achieved a circulation of nearly forty-two millions a year against an American circulation of over eighty-six millions. Canada . . . is the only country of any size in the world . . . whose people read more foreign periodicals than they do periodicals published in their own land, local newspapers excluded.

The fare of Canadian moviegoers is much the same as that of their southern neighbors—overwhelmingly made-in-Hollywood. The most popular radio and television programs among Canadians originate in New York.

The same impact is seen at work in the socio-economic sphere. By far the greatest number of household appliances and auto-

[8] From "Canada's Besieged Culture," article by Otto Butz, political scientist at Princeton University *Antioch Review*. 16:91-101. Spring 1956. Article first published in *Antioch Review*. Reprinted by permission.

mobiles purchased by Canadians bear the same names as those which have become embedded in the American way of life. They are either imported from the United States or manufactured by Canadian subsidiaries of American firms. Nor is there any difference in the prestige-rating which the society assigns to these various commodities. Men of distinction prefer the same brands of whiskey. The Canadian who has "arrived" drives a Cadillac. Seven-tenths of Canada's 1.3 million organized workers are members of the Trades and Labor Congress and the Canadian Congress of Labor, affiliates of the AFL-CIO. The standards of wages and working conditions demanded by Canadian labor generally are those which at any given time are being achieved south of the border. In arguing a wage dispute before a conciliation board, for example, the CIO United Steel Workers of Hamilton, Ontario, . . . made the statement, in support of their demands, that Canada, and especially the province of Ontario, is economically just as much part of the United States as Texas.

And while this cultural invasion *from* the United States continues and grows in dimensions and intensity with increasing Canadian urbanization and rising standards of living, Canada's potential for building up a competing cultural nucleus of its own, it is felt, remains seriously weakened by the attraction of much of the country's best professional and artistic talent *to* the United States. If a Canadian student wishes the advantages of high caliber advanced studies he must usually do his graduate work abroad. Whereas in generations past it was fashionable to spend the necessary years at Oxford or Cambridge, the schools selected today are predominantly in the United States. Moreover, the "Ivy League" has the same connotation in Canada today as it has had by tradition in the United States. As a result, it is estimated, Canada "sells down south" as many as 2,500 professional men and women a year. And the situation in the area of the creative arts is little different. . . .

How are Canadians attempting to account for, and cope with this situation? One type of response has been that of the federal government. For years now, and especially since the publication of the findings of the Royal Commission, Ottawa has been engaged in a campaign to augment aid to higher education, to find ways of improving and supplementing the performance of the government-operated Canadian Broadcasting Corporation, and to provide greater financial and promotional encouragement for work in the arts, letters and sciences generally. The other principal type of response has been the unofficial one of Canada's intellectuals. By approaching Canadian culture in terms of its various component parts, these latter are at work attempting to show why and how in each regard Canadian culture is weak, and to suggest ways in which, in each writer's particular field of competence, the situation might be reconstituted so as to contribute to the greater originality, impregnability and power of attraction of Canadian culture as a whole. . . .

That . . . [a] potential for cultural achievements of internationally recognized caliber exists in Canada cannot be doubted. But what are the prospects that the potential will unfold as a national Canadian culture and not, as seems already to be occurring, as various merely regional expressions of a continental American culture? Is the will to develop a distinctive Canadian culture going to be enough? Does Canada possess the necessary matrix or nucleus for the building of such a culture? Is not this the problem, this absence of a native Canadian idiom, which lies at the core of the inadequacies which Canadians see in their art and literature and intellectual life?

That Canada's position in this regard is not strong most thoughtful Canadians are prepared to agree. Their politico-philosophical roots, they know, are like those of the United States embedded in the victorious struggles for liberal democratic principles fought in seventeenth-century England. But they know too that, unlike the United States, their origins as a nation cannot be identified with any one outstanding act of defiance of a common enemy either by bloodshed or by eloquent appeal to universal truth. There is no Canadian national myth. . . . Canada has no George Washington, nor a "Constitution" in the American sense. Canadians consider their institutions and processes of government with admirable pragmatism. While this saves them from some of the excesses which characterize the American political scene, it at the same time deprives them of one of the most compelling elements that go into the making of a distinctive national cultural core.

But, it may be asked, what about French Canada? Does not this section of Canada and its heritage constitute a valuable ingredient of a common, native cultural nucleus? While well-intentioned Canadians have had many hopeful things to say on this subject, it is generally recognized that the answer can, at best, be a "yes" that must be severely qualified. For one thing, English-speaking Canadians consider their national culture to be essentially of a dual nature. Even if it were a possibility, they would resist a cultural merging with French Canada to the utmost. And the French Canadians, for their part, are even more sharply jealous of their distinctive identity. Their traditional clerical-agricultural order is fast falling prey to the inroads of industrialization and urbanization. Because of their past concentration on the professions of the priesthood, law and medicine, and because of their lack of capital, the new economic developments are in large part being financed and technically and administratively directed by English-Canadians and Americans. This is making the process of adjusting to the twentieth century all the more painful. And while indications are that most French Canadians can be expected eventually to accept increasing economic and political integration with the rest of Canada, and through it with English-speaking North America as a whole, it seems no less probable that a minority will offer the most tenacious resistance. . . .

But if, then, neither its French-Canadian component nor its political heritage seem of a nature such as decisively to serve the desired national purpose, can Canada at least rely on its traditional British core as a mold and a synthesizing force in the evolution of a native culture? The reply, many Canadians will reluctantly agree, must once again be essentially negative. The influence of the British-colonial, Tory elite, which once set the social and intellectual standards in Canada, is being rapidly reduced both by shifts to a more American-type outlook on life within its own ranks as well as by rejection of its claims to pre-eminence by the Canadian people as a whole. Thus, for ex-

ample, to quote . . . from Professor Lower's discussion of Canadian universities,

> Students . . . turn increasingly away, not only from the history of Europe
> but from the history of England. Give them American history and they
> respond at once. . . . Time begins in North America. . . . I myself am
> firmly convinced that in education the customer is invariably wrong;
> nevertheless I suppose by sheer weight of numbers he will eventually
> secure the goods he thinks he wants. And the traditional goods, our
> cultural inheritance, become harder and harder to sell.

While it still might be objected that this tide might yet be
turned by extensive enough immigration from the United Kingdom, the fact is that of the one million newcomers to Canada
since 1945, only thirty-five per cent have been British. And even
for these, not to speak of the remainder, attachment to the new
homeland only rarely consists of patriotic identification with
Canada as a traditional British nation. Much more common is
the attitude that Canada is simply a land of welcome opportunity,
the closest one can get to the ideal of "America" without actually
being admitted across the United States border. That these so-
called "New Canadians" will serve to improve the prospects of
a distinctive Canadian national culture therefore seems highly
doubtful. What appears more likely is that they will increase
Canada's receptiveness to American influences even further.

While many Canadians appear to recognize these weaknesses
in Canada's potential for the development of a national culture,
very few of them are prepared to go so far as to conclude that
the situation is hopeless and that the objective should be given
up altogether. . . .

The Canadian writer, Lister Sinclair, for example, in a discussion of the works of the country's youngest generation of
literary figures, ("The Canadian Idiom," *Here and Now,* June
1949.) sees new hope for Canada's autonomous cultural future
in the fact that

> all these people are united by one thing: they are experts in the use of
> the still small voice. That is to say, the literary device they have in
> common is that of *irony.* . . . This they are beginning to discover is the
> essence of the Canadian spirit, that it is that enables them to handle
> contradictions. . . . It was the weapon of Socrates, and has been the

weapon of many good men since. The principle of letting the giants destroy one another by their strength is making Canada's weakness into still greater strength.

Although such attempts to enthrone the retreat to irony are understandable, they would hardly seem to represent the type of basic orientation from which there could develop a fruitful culture—whether national or any other kind. Rather, they appear to express a counsel of irresponsibility and moral abdication. If taken seriously they would not only further hasten the American cultural absorption of the Canadian people but would soon make of Canada a provincial cultural backwater. Not only politically, but culturally as well, Canada is inescapably an integral part of the twentieth-century world. While Canadian intellectuals may be appalled by some of the characteristics of this world and frustrated by their undeniably limited power significantly to affect them, their flight into irony would not only leave the situation unchanged but would limit their effectiveness even further.

DEFROSTING CANADIAN CULTURE [9]

Such national unity as Canada possesses is the result of an east-west railway which was rushed into being by the government to prevent American infiltration of the western territories. The enormously expensive and unprofitable railway system thus constructed was more of a political gesture than an economic speculation. It naturally led to the negotiation of trade agreements with England to foster east-west movements of goods to pay for the railways. But the natural economic movement of goods on this continent tends to be north-south rather than east-west, with the result that the Canadian economy is an artificial one, and subject to severe internal strains. . . .

The French-English division in Canada has coincided with the natural geographic weakness of official east-west unity. And the natural north-south alignment is seen in the fact that

[9] From article by Marshall MacLuhan of the University of Toronto. *American Mercury.* 74:91-7. March 1952. Reprinted by permission.

there are nearly as many French who have moved to New England as there are left in Quebec itself. Moreover, there has been a steady flow of Canadians from Nova Scotia and New Brunswick to the States in the past century, so that, for several reasons, those provinces have long regarded Boston as their cultural capital. The predominantly Scottish complexion of the Canadian eastern seaboard (the Maritimes) has developed a culture which clashes openly with "English" Ontario. So, naturally, the Maritimer or "Blue-Nose," in his westward migrations from industry-starved Nova Scotia and New Brunswick, by-passes Ontario in favor of the western provinces. And the Scot, with his caution and his sentiment, his passion for education and economy, dominates Canadian universities, banking, and law. The Scot has given not only stability but a dour and cagey tone to Canadian life as surely as the Irish have contributed to the gaiety, vivacity, and instability of feeling in the United States.

Ontario itself, constituting so much of Canada, yet representing neither the parts to the east or west of it, is ideologically split by many historic causes which are still active. Its numerous religious and political factions (arising from various strata of immigration) have left a heritage of suspicion which is gradually being dissipated as industrial prosperity obliterates the past and puts the population into confident motion. But the volume and tempo of Canadian economic life has only recently got to the point which in the United States has long taught people to live in the present. Nevertheless, Canada is still as historically-minded as the American South, with which it has so much in common.

The Canadian West is the antithesis of Ontario in being socially homogeneous and egalitarian. The conditions of life there at first put everybody on an equal footing, and the attitude remains. Yet, in spite of the fact that westerners are socially more "American" than the rest of Canada, their old-country sentiment is very strong, due mainly to the Scottish influence [of the Maritimers who went West].

The cultural shadow which for centuries England cast over the arts on this side of the Atlantic has vanished. Instead,

American arts are blanketing English intellectual life just as American movies have for two decades been providing English children with new speech habits. There is no longer any excuse for the immigrant humility in artistic matters which for so long pervaded American cultural life.

For Canadians as colonials, this blighting humility in intellectual and artistic life has been even more continuously and intensely felt than in the United States. For it was a matter of loyalty to foster and taste it. . . .

Actually, the very absence of cluttering example and tradition in the arts is the main Canadian opportunity. The only possible strategy for the Canadian writer, poet, artist (as it was for Joyce, Pound, and Eliot when they found themselves in cultural back-waters) is to conquer the old traditions through the most revolutionary artistic techniques suggested by the current modes of science and technology. This is the really great advantage enjoyed by any provincial in a time of rapid change. He cannot come to the new through the old, but must discover and master the old through what is most recent. By the very nature of his situation, he is familiar with the new and somewhat at a loss in the presence of the traditional. . . .

The Canadian, located between two great communities, the English and the American, is provincial to both. He would, therefore, be in a superb position to develop habits of critical insight if the development of such habits were not paralyzed by colonial timidity or Scottish caution.

As a frontier territory Canada has become increasingly attractive as a site for American investments and as an indispensable source of raw materials for American heavy industry. The water power, pulp, and iron ore of Quebec have recently led to such a massive invasion of American capital that the old province is undergoing a sort of accelerated industrial revolution.

This development suggests various reflections. Economically speaking, the French in Canada have always been second-class citizens beside the commercially-minded Scotch and English. But culturally speaking, the French have always regarded the English as interlopers—not really Canadians—and as materialistic Babbitts. Therefore, in intellectual and artistic affairs French

Canada outranks the larger English-speaking community. The French have produced more and better poets, novelists, critics, and musicians. Their intellectuals were nourished by a nineteenth century which in France was as unmistakably first-rate as the later Victorian period in England was second-rate. That is why English Canada today is still Victorian in its "serious" culture and contemporary only insofar as it absorbs unconsciously the entertainment of the American mass-media. But the French in Canada are not handicapped by the same measure of culture-lag which in English Canada creates acute indigestion in the presence of the art and thought of a technological world.

The question arises as to what will be the effect on Canada of a superior French esthetic culture if it should suddenly be provided with an economic base at least equal to that of Ontario? Will French-Canadian culture survive prosperity and technology? Will its language survive the greatly increased demands for spoken English which arise with the increased commerce with the United States?

The Royal Commission report on Canadian culture looks wistfully at the French language bulwark against American culture. Ottawa is not at all averse to finding some bureaucratic equivalent for that French language barrier to the infiltration of American entertainment. But the Royal Commission, while distressed over the plight of Canadian painters, writers, and musicians who must compete for attention on unequal terms with their American colleagues, has not yet achieved an adequate working analysis of the culture of this continent or this century.

The Royal Commission is squarely in line with our bureaucrats and Victorian patriarchs in supposing that culture is basically an unpleasant moral duty. According to this view, everything that people do spontaneously and with gusto, everything connected with industry, commerce, sport, and popular entertainment is merely vulgar. . . . But modern anthropology and sociology have begun to open up new conceptions in these matters. . . . [Canadians] have reached the end of the Gutenberg era of the printed word before, as Canadians, they have had anything very important to print. They are, therefore, free to exploit the new media without the exhausting effort of self-extrication from the old.

Once Canadians adopt that attitude they will drop their defensive tactics against the "threat" from English and American culture and welcome such contacts.

UNITY VIA VIDEO [10]

In our opinion . . . broadcasting, be it radio or television, should meet the following basic requirements.

(1) There should be at least one national system. This system should be concerned with the nation as a whole and not just a segment of that, be the segment local, regional or special interest.

(2) It is imperative, at this time in our history, that this system, or systems, work adequately towards a fuller understanding on the part of all Canadians, of other Canadians and other Canadian areas, their characteristics, their problems and their aspirations, and through this to a greater sense of nationhood. In like manner broadcasting should impart similar information and knowledge of other countries and other people, and international affairs generally. Broadcasting can and should be a great never-ending people's university, providing both education and entertainment, frequently simultaneously, thus increasing the height and breadth of the minds of the Canadian people, their knowledge, their understanding and their capacity for critical thinking.

(3) Broadcasting must assume its own strategic and peculiar role of responsibility for not only the preservation but the extension of the ideas and concepts of human dignity, human and civil rights, individual worth, the rule of law and not of man, free parliamentary and other governmental and nongovernmental institutions and all those other things which we gather under the umbrella term "Democracy." Any system, be it public

[10] From article entitled "Canadian Broadcasting Policy." *Citizenship Items* (bulletin issued by Canadian Citizenship Council). 9:5-6. May-June 1958. Reprinted by permission.

or private, that does not give adequate attention to these things is in effect an enemy of democracy, by design or omission. . . .

To date Canada has managed to work out a compromise between two extremes which has given us, for peculiar needs and circumstances of our country, a fairly well balanced program of broadcasting fare, both as to content and quality of presentation. We probably have the best balanced system in the world today. That many of our programs are of high quality is confirmed by the many international awards won by Canadian programs. . . .

It is pretty obvious that if we are going to have the variety and quality of content and of presentation which will aid in the growth of mature and responsible democratic citizens, much of the responsibility for this will fall upon the public system, namely the CBC [Canadian Broadcasting Corporation]. While there are many examples of private stations, both radio and television, and of advertising-supported programs, providing something better, and in some cases much better than the usual mass appealing fare, the past experience as far as we have been able to ascertain, in Canada, in the United States and in Britain, has been that this type of a program has been the occasional exception, and it is not likely that advertising-supported programs would provide adequate balance and variety in a day or a week or a month's program.

It will be necessary, therefore, for the public body to be supplied with sufficient financial resources to ensure that its sustaining programs do provide sufficient balance to the whole system or systems. And as time goes on the present guesses of the CBC Board of Governors may prove to be very modest and conservative rather than exorbitant.

One of these guesses is that by 1961 CBC will cost $150 million a year. At the present time we are spending nearly fifteen times that amount in providing men and machines to destroy the bodies of an enemy should we again be faced with war. And yet it has been stated time and time again that the real world struggle is for men's minds. Only an adult nation, strong in the understanding of our concepts of freedom and democracy, can stand up to this war for men's minds. Consequently it is our view that the expenditure on the CBC to enable it in a variety of ways to strengthen and increase the maturity and democratic fiber of the Canadian people is an expenditure of equal importance to that of national defense.

Broadcasting, and particularly television, is a medium of such tremendous and far-reaching power and influence on the thinking and the feelings of people that it is imperative that it not be permitted to get into the hands of any segment of the Canadian people, or persons other than the Canadian people, to be used for their own selfish interests rather than in the interest of the nation as a whole.

It may not be entirely inconceivable that the ultimate control of broadcasting in Canada might fall in one of three places: (1) The Parliament of Canada—where it theoretically rests now; (2) the federal political party in power—where some people feel that it in fact rests now, or (3) the large corporations capable of using broadcasting as a national advertising media, both Canadian and American.

It is absolutely imperative that broadcasting control and the control of policy and content does not rest with that segment of the Canadian people, and some of the American counterparts, whose one purpose of using broadcasting is to sell their products to the most number of people. We reject all arguments favoring the use of broadcasting as solely and primarily an advertising sheet, with control of policy and content subject to the specific needs of the advertisers.

Until fairly recently, with the exception of French-speaking Canada, we had little in the way of a distinctive Canadian philosophy or culture, the soul and the manifestations of the soul of a nation. But such is now beginning to emerge. And as it grows and flourishes, so will the strength and health and unity of our Canadian people.

For too long we have been users of second-hand ideas; ideas growing out of climate and circumstances other than Canadian. If our nation is to grow as a nation and a people, then its ideas must be largely indigenous.

No other nation, to our knowledge, is so subjected to the "dumping" of foreign ideas. It has been claimed that more than 80 per cent of periodicals read by Canadians are foreign. We understand that approximately 40 per cent of the programs on the English TV are foreign, many of them at the best viewing hours. Radio, we understand in this new age of TV is now largely Canadian, although a high percentage of this is recordings by American artists.

Not for one moment do we suggest that all Canadian radio and television should be Canadian material produced by Canadians. As a young nation and people we need the knowledge, stimulation and experience of the best from other countries, programming that will give us further understanding of the peoples and problems of other countries—what they think, how they feel, what they do, how they live, what they enjoy —and provide a dynamic montage or scales of ideas, tastes and values that will provide stimulation and focus and clarity to Canadian ideas and tastes and values.

We view with grave concern the accumulative effect of the daily massive "dumping" of foreign ideas via the mass media, largely from one source, and the proselytizing of these ideas being paid for by Canadians to the detriment of the creation and growth of Canadian ideas. We can never become a true nation and a real people if our tastes and values are merely second-hand, astigmatic carbon copies of those of another nation, we must be ourselves.

Any changes in the policies, the organization, the financing and the administration of broadcasting in Canada should be to lessen the present imbalance, and to broaden by content and source, foreign programs in Canada.

PROMOTING CANADIAN TALENT [11]

With its immense expanse of territory and its small and scattered population of seventeen million, Canada has had particular problems to overcome in bringing the arts to its people.

[11] From article entitled "Canada Council Helps Subsidize The Arts," by Tania Long. New York *Times*. p7-9. September 7, 1958. Reprinted by permission.

The physical facilities needed for the arts to flourish—the theatres, concert halls—are still largely lacking. Even Ottawa, the capital, has neither, and as a result is bypassed by visiting theatrical companies traveling to Montreal and Toronto on their North American tours.

It was to help overcome these handicaps, as well as to foster the education of artists, social scientists and humanists that the Canada Council was created by the government from a windfall of large death duties paid by the estates of two Canadian millionaires. The council was given $100 million to be divided into two $50 million funds. One was an endowment fund, the annual income of which is used in scholarships, grants and special fellowships for graduate study. The other sum is to be used up in a period of about ten years in capital grants to universities for new buildings which will be used in teaching the arts, humanities and social sciences.

The endowment fund grants handed out during the past season, after a cautious study of the many applications that poured in, already have shown a solid benefit to the organizations assisted. This season's grants, which are bigger than last season's, can be expected to carry these benefits further.

The Ottawa Philharmonic Orchestra is an example of how orchestras gained, as a result of Canada Council help. By assisting the orchestra to move from an amateur to a semiprofessional basis, the council helped create a far finer symphonic instrument, which in turn drew bigger crowds and ended up the year in the black for the first time in its recent history.

The council's first annual report, which was issued late this summer, sheds an interesting light on the interrelation of council grants and public attendance. During the first year, the Canada Council contributed about one eighth of total receipts to the orchestras. Attendance, throughout the country, however, increased by one half.

It is the council's policy of adding to but not replacing local financial support for the various artistic endeavors it assists. Its officers were gratified to note that in many cases community support was increased as a consequence of council grants.

There is another aspect in which council assistance is proving significant. By providing more employment for musicians in Canada, as well as higher pay, it keeps Canadian musicians within the country instead of crossing into the United States for jobs.

BIBLIOGRAPHY

An asterisk (*) preceding a reference indicates that the article or a part of it has been reprinted in this book.

BOOKS AND PAMPHLETS

*American Council on Education. Report of the Canada-United States Conference on Mutual Relations, Washington, D.C., February 7-8, 1955. 71p. The Council. 1785 Massachusetts Ave. Washington 6, D.C. '55.

Barber, Joseph. Good fences make good neighbors; why the United States provokes Canadians. 280p. Bobbs-Merrill Co. New York. '59.

*Barkway, Michael. Turning point for immigration? (Behind The Headlines. v 17, no4). 16p. Canadian Institute of International Affairs. 230 Bloor St. W. Toronto, Ont. '57.

Bissell, C. T. Canada's crisis in higher education. 272p. University of Toronto Press. Toronto, Ont. '57.

Bissell, C. T., ed. Our living tradition: seven Canadians. 113p. University of Toronto Press. Toronto, Ont. '57.

*Brady, Alexander. Cooperation is imperative; background paper prepared for Canadian Institute of International Affairs. 3p. mimeo. The Institute. 230 Bloor St. W. Toronto, Ont. no date.

Brown, G. W., ed. Canada. (United Nations Series) 621p. University of California Press. Berkeley. '50.

Brown, G. W. Growth of peaceful settlement between Canada and the United States. (Contemporary Affairs no22). 40p. Ryerson Press. Toronto, Ont. '48.

*Bryden, Ken. What is the CCF? 16p. Cooperative Commonwealth Federation. 301 Metcalfe Street. Ottawa, Ont. '55.

Burt, A. L. Short history of Canada for Americans. 309p. University of Minnesota Press. Minneapolis. '44.

Canada. Department of External Affairs. Information Division. Canadian system of education. 17p. Ottawa, Ont. '56.

*Canada. Department of External Affairs. Information Division. Fact sheet no4. The Department. Ottawa, Ont. Je. '57.

*Canada. Department of External Affairs. Information Division. Fact sheet no5. The Department. Ottawa, Ont. Je. '57.

Canada. Department of Labour. Economics and research bureau. Working and living conditions in Canada. 40p. Queen's Printer. Ottawa, Ont. '55.

Canada. Dominion Bureau of Statistics. Information Services Division. Canada Year Book. Queen's Printer. Ottawa, Ont.
This report, published annually, is an invaluable source of information on Canada.

*Canadian Association for Adult Education. Has Canada an independent foreign policy? (Citizen's Forum Pamphlet no 14) The Association. 113 St. George St. Toronto 5, Ont. '57.

Canadian Broadcasting Corporation. Twenty-five years of Canadian foreign policy. 87p. The Corporation. 354 Jarvis Street. Toronto, Ont.

Canadian Citizenship Council. Immigration and population growth. 24p. The Council. 180 Bay Street. Ottawa, Ont. '56.

Canadian Welfare Council. Public welfare developments in Canada, 1954-55. 43p. The Council. 55 Parkdale. Ottawa, Ont. '56.

Center for Information on America. How about Canada and the U.S.? (Future Voters Discussion Guide. v4, no 1) 4p. The Center. Washington, Conn. '54.

Central Office of Information. Reference Division. Commonwealth in brief. 120p. London. '57.

Central Office of Information. Reference Division. Constitutional development in the Commonwealth. London. '57.

Chapin, Miriam. Contemporary Canada. 337p. Oxford University Press. New York. '58.

Clokie, H. M. Canadian government and politics. rev. ed. 370p. Longmans, Green & Co. New York. '51.

Corey, A. B. Canadian-American relations along the Detroit river. 24p. Wayne State University Press. Detroit, Mich. '57.

Costain, T. B. High towers. 403p. Doubleday & Co. New York. '49.

Costain, T. B. White and the gold; the French regime in Canada. 482p. Doubleday & Co. New York. '54.

Creighton, D. G. History of Canada; dominion of the North. rev. and enl. ed. 619p. Houghton Mifflin Co. Boston. '58.

Dales, J. H. Canada's energy prospects. (Behind The Headlines. v. 17, no2). 16p. Canadian Institute of International Affairs. 230 Bloor Street W. Toronto, Ont. '57.

Dauphinee, John. Opportunity in Canada. 2d ed. 286p. Rockliff Publishing Corp. London. '58.

Dowling, P. M. Challenge of Saskatchewan's future. 6p. Stanford Research Institute. Public relations office. Menlo Park, Calif. '56.

Flaherty, Frank. Freedom of the press in Canada. (Buchanan's Bulletin) 16p. 53 Queen Street, Ottawa, Ont. '57.

Gibson, J. D., ed. Canada's economy in a changing world. 380p. St. Martin's Press. New York. '48.

Gilmour, G. P., ed. Canada's tomorrow. 324p. St. Martin's Press. New York. '54.

Glazebrook, G. P. de T. History of Canadian external relations. 449p. Oxford University Press. New York. '51.

Glazebrook, G. P. de T. Short history of Canada. 238p. Oxford University Press. New York. '50.

Government of Canada. Canada and the United Nations. 1954-55. (Conference Series 1956) 118p. Queen's Printer. Ottawa, Ont. '56.

Government of Canada. Parliament of Canada. 22p. Queen's Printer. Ottawa, Ont. no date.

*Hills, Theo L. Canada. (Focus Series. v9, no5) 6p. American Geographical Society. Broadway at 156th St. New York 32. '59.

Hosken, William. Economic aspects of industrial development of northern Canada. 8p. Stanford Research Institute. Public relations office. Menlo Park, Calif. '57.

Hughes, E. C. French Canada in transition. 227p. University of Chicago Press. Chicago. '43.

Hutchison, Bruce. Canada: tomorrow's giant. 325p. Alfred A. Knopf. New York. '57.

Hutchison, Bruce. Incredible Canadian; a candid portrait of Mackenzie King; his works, his times, and his nation. 454p. Longmans, Green & Co. New York. '53.

Hutchison, Bruce. Struggle for the border. 500p. Longmans, Green & Co. New York. '55.

Interprovincial Farm Union Council. Rise and fall of Canadian farm organizations. 119p. 416 Main Street. Winnipeg, Manitoba. '55.

Jamieson, Stuart. Industrial relations in Canada. (Studies in International Labor) 144p. Cornell University Press. Ithaca, N.Y. '57.

Keenleyside, H. L. Canada and the United States. rev. and enl. ed. 406p. Alfred A. Knopf. New York. '52.

Kent, Tom. American boom in Canada. (Winnipeg Free Press Pamphlet no55) 16p. Winnipeg Free Press. Winnipeg, Manitoba. '57.

Kent, Tom. Liberal economics and Canadian federation. (Winnipeg Free Press Pamphlet no54) 14p. Winnipeg Free Press. Winnipeg, Manitoba. '56.

Korns, W. A. Relations with Canada. (Editorial Research Reports. v. 1, no20) 20p. 1156 19th Street. Washington 6, D.C. '57.

Laugharne, Grace. Canada looks ahead. 158p. Oxford University Press. New York. '56.

Le Bourdais, D. M. Canada's century. 214p. Frederick A. Praeger. New York. '52.

Le Bourdais, D. M. Nation of the north; Canada since confederation. 270p. Frederick A. Praeger. New York. '53.

McInnis, Edgar. Canada; a political and social history. 574p. Rinehart & Co. New York. '57.

Mantley, John. Snowbirch. 316p. E. P. Dutton & Co. New York. '58. Novel set in northern Canada.

Mercer, G. A. Province of Newfoundland. 32p. Canadian geographical society. Ottawa, Ont. '57.

Miner, Horace. St. Denis: a French-Canadian parish. 283p. University of Chicago Press. Chicago. '39.

Municipality of Metropolitan Toronto. Metropolitan Toronto. 36p. City Hall. Toronto, Ont. '57.

Neuberger, R. L. Royal Canadian mounted police. 182p. Random House. New York. '53.

Nicholson, N. L. Boundaries of Canada, its provinces and territories. 142p. Canadian Department of Mines and Technical Surveys. Queen's Printer. Ottawa, Ont. '54.

Park, Julian, ed. Culture of contemporary Canada. 404p. Cornell University Press. Ithaca, N.Y. '57.

*Pearson, Lester B. Crown and the Commonwealth; address delivered at the University of Oregon, May 25, 1953. mimeo. Department of External Affairs. Information Division. Ottawa, Ont. '53.

Phillips, Alan. Living legend; story of the Royal Canadian mounted police. 328p. Little, Brown. Boston. '57.

Raddall, T. H. Path of destiny; Canada from the British conquest to home rule, 1763-1850. Doubleday & Co. New York. '57.

Ross, F. A. Land and people of Canada. 128p. J. B. Lippincott Co. Philadelphia. '54.

Roy, Gabrielle. Tin flute. 315p. Harcourt, Brace & Co. New York. '47.
    Novel of a large French-Canadian family living in Montreal during the depression.

Royal Bank of Canada. Public health. (Monthly Letter. v37, no2) 4p. The Bank. Montreal, Que. '56.

Scotton, C. A. Brief history of Canadian labor. Cooperative Commonwealth Federation. 301 Metcalfe Street. Ottawa, Ont. '56.

Seagram, J. E. and sons. Awakening North. 29p. 1430 Peel Street. Montreal, Que. '56.

Seagram, J. E. and sons. Awakening North. 29p. The Publisher? 1430 Peel Street. Montreal, Que. '56.

Shaw, L. W. Province of Prince Edward Island, Canada. 32p. Canadian Geographical Society. Ottawa, Ont. '57.

Simpson, R. A. Province of Nova Scotia. 32p. Canadian Geographical Society. Ottawa, Ont. '57.

Soward, F. H. and McInnis, E. W. Canada and the United Nations. 285p. Manhattan Publishing Co. New York. '57.

*Spencer, R. A. Canadian foreign policy: conservative style. (Behind The Headlines. v 18, no3) 16p. Canadian Institute of International Affairs. 230 Bloor St. W. Toronto, Ont. '58.

Spicer, Bart. Tall captains. 538p. Dodd, Mead & Co. New York. '57.
    Novel about New France.

Stanley, G. F. G., with H. M. Jackson. Canada's soldiers, 1604-1954; the military history of an unmilitary people. 401p. St. Martin's Press. New York. '54.

Twitty, Tom and Wade, Mason. Canada, a great small power. (Headline Series no 103) 62p. Foreign Policy Association. New York. '54.

*United States Chamber of Commerce. Our partnership with Canada. (Information Bulletin no34) 8p. The Chamber. Information Department. 1615 H St. Washington 6, D.C. '54.

Wade, Mason. French Canadians, 1760-1945. 1136p. Macmillan Co. New York. '55.

Watkins, Ernest. Prospect of Canada. 271p. Secker and Warburg. London. '54.

Watson, J. W. Land of Canada. 32p. Canadian Geographical Society. Ottawa, Ont. '56.

White, C. L. Regional geography of Anglo-America. 2d ed. 518p. Prentice-Hall. New York. '54.

Wilson, Clifford. North of 55°; Canada from the 55th parallel to the Pole. 190p. Ryerson Press. Toronto, Ont. '54.

Woodsworth, C. J. Canadian policies in Asia. 45p. Institute of Pacific Relations. 1 E. 54th St. New York 22. '54.

*Wrong, Dennis. American and Canadian viewpoints. 62p. American Council on Education. Washington, D.C. '55.

PERIODICALS

*America. 97:189-91. My. 11, '57. Family allowances. Richard L. Neuberger.

*America. 97:226-8. My. 18, '57. Canada's new stature. Neil McKenty.

*America. 98:276-7. N. 30, '57. The DEW Line; radar frontier. S. G. Kehoe.

*America. 99:349-50. Je. 21, '58. Canadian church in flux. J. E. Belliveau.

America. 99:392-3. Jl. 5, '58. Will Canada have a labor party? E. L. Chicanot.

American Economic Review. 47:596-609; 613-14. My. '57. United States capital investments in Canada [with discussion]. F. A. Knox.

*American Mercury. 74:91-7. Mr. '52. Defrosting Canadian culture. H. M. MacLuhan.

Annals of the American Academy of Political and Social Science. 316: 18-24. Mr. '58. Reproductive renaissance north of the Rio Grande. N. B. Ryder.

*Annals of the American Academy of Political and Social Science. 316: 34-43. Mr. '58. United States and Canada: magnets for immigration. H. F. Eckerson.

Annals of the American Academy of Political and Social Science. 316: 60-8. Mr. '58. Urban and metropolitan development in the United States and Canada. Leo F. Schnore and G. B. Peterson.

*Antioch Review. 16:91-101. Spring '56. Canada's beseiged culture. Otto Butz.

Atlantic Monthly. 199:37-40. Mr. '57. Canadian looks us over. J. H. Gray.

*Atlantic Monthly. 201:18-23. Je. '58. The Atlantic Report: Canada.

Business Week. p70-3+. Ag. 6, '55. Alberta's oil builds a Canadian Texas.

Business Week. p66+. O. 1, '55. Making room for the Seaway, a reluctant town moves on.

Business Week. p61-2+. Mr. 16, '57. Wenner-Gren's $1-billion baby.

Business Week. p 187. Jl. 8, '57. Elite of about 100 men guide Canada's whole economy, professor says.

Business Week. p28-9. Jl. 19, '58. Canada heads to health.

Canadian Journal of Economics and Political Science. 23:376-84. Ag. '57. Economic elite and the social structure. John Porter.

Canadian Journal of Economics and Political Science. 23:504-15. N. '57. Quebec and Canadian democracy. M. Oliver.

Canadian Journal of Economics and Political Science. 23:540-9. N. '57. Ethnic assimilation and differentiation in Canada. Frank G. Vallee and others.

Canadian Journal of Economics and Political Science. 24:9-20. F. '58. Demographic trends in Canada, 1941-56, and some of their implications. A. H. Le Neveu and Y. Kasahara.

Canadian Journal of Economics and Political Science. 24:70-83. F. '58. Movement toward labour unity in Canada, history and implications. E. Forsey.

Canadian Journal of Economics and Political Science. 24:102-3. F. '58. Canada's birth-rate. H. H. Aschmann and H. G. J. Aitken.

Canadian Journal of Economics and Political Science. 24:104-10. F. '58. Canada's economic prospects. H. G. Johnson.

Christian Century. 73:55-6. Ja. 11, '56. Prairie Canada studies itself. H. R. Lane.

Christian Century. 73:1125-6. O. 3, '56. Church grows in Canada. H. E. Fey.

Christian Century. 73:1508-10. D. 26, '56. Canada no chore boy. J. R. Mutchmor.

Christian Century. 74:219. F. 20, '57. Education vital to Canada's future.

*Christian Century. 74:680-1. My. 29, '57. Canada's federal election. J. R. Mutchmor.

Christian Century. 74:1030. S. 4, '57. Canada is Canadian.

Christian Century. 75:46-8. Ja. 8, '58. Census and the churches. T. Donnelly.

Citizenship Items (Canadian Citizenship Council). 9:6-7. Mr.-Ap. '58. Labour and immigration; where should immigration be?

*Citizenship Items (Canadian Citizenship Council). 9:5-6. My.-Je. '58. Canadian broadcasting policy.

Commonweal. 62:308-9. Je. 24, '55. Review of H. M. Wade's *French Canadians, 1760-1945.* M. Lavanoux.

Commonweal. 68:443-5. Ag. 1, '58. Anti-Americanism in Canada? J. E. Belliveau.

Current History. Jl. '55. Canada [entire issue].

Economist. 179:161-2. Ap. 14, '56. Canada's Maritime provinces.

*Economist. 181:981-2. D. 15, '56. Canada: a bird's eye view; growing pains of a young giant.

*Economist. 181:1135-6. D. 29, '56. Bird's eye view of Canada—II; where Malthus is no prophet.

Economist. 183:802. Je. 1, '57. Canada and the younger sisters.

Economist. 183:1071. Je. 22, '57. Canada and the Commonwealth.

Economist. 184:370. Ag. 3, '57. Damming the flood.

*Economist. 184:390-1. Ag. 3, '57. Plastic igloo.

Economist. 185:218+. O. 19, '57. Best neighbor policy.

Economist. 185:229-30. O. 19, '57. Queen in Canada; a Canadian monarchy; Mr. Diefenbaker's program.

*Economist. 185:504+. N. 9, '57. Canada's social conscience.

Economist. 186:44. Ja. 4, '58. Canada: the candid ally.

Economist. 187:220+. Ap. 19, '58. Any future for Social Credit?

Foreign Affairs. 34:117-27. O. '55. Canadian economy and its competitors. W. A. Mackintosh.

Foreign Affairs. 35:581-92. Jl. '57. Changing place of Canada. Tom Kent.

Foreign Affairs. 36:409-17. Ap. '58. Canada rediscovers its history. M. Barkway.

Foreign Affairs. 36:633-44. Jl. '58. Massive alternation in Canadian politics. Steve Muller.

Fortune. 56:281-2+. S. '57. Canada's black-golden West; West-coast transmission.

Harper's Magazine. 215:42-9. D. '57. Power struggle on the Canadian border. R. L. Neuberger.

Harper's Magazine. 216:46-50. My. '58. Why Canadians are turning anti-American. B. Hutchison.

House Beautiful. 101:84+. Mr. '59. Canada, a giant land of unexpected pleasure. M. Gough.

Life. 39:63-4. S. 12, '55. Evangeline's children gather.

Nation. 181:257-9. S. 24, '55. Revolt in Quebec. Ross Harkness.

Nation. 183:280-3. O. 6, '56. Conquest of Canada. M. Gayn.

Negro History Bulletin. 18:105-6. F. '55. Negro-white relations in western Ontario. R. D. Wilson.

New Republic. 136:9-10. Ap. 29, '57. Canada-U.S. inevitable allies. P. Deane.

New Statesman and Nation. 52:443-4. O. 13, '56. Notes on an under-developed country. R. H. S. Crossman.
  Reply. 52:519. O. 27, 56. A. Martin.
*New York Times. sec 11. p 1. Je. 29, '58. What the Seaway is. P. J. C. Friedlander.
*New York Times. sec 11. p 16. Je. 29, '58. Labrador's ore to aid Seaway. Clark Davey.
*New York Times. sec 11. p21. Je. 29, '58. Frontier of understanding. Raymond Daniell.
*New York Times. sec 2. p7. S. 7, '58. Canada Council helps subsidize the arts. Tania Long.
New York Times Magazine. p 17+. Mr. 25, '56. Portrait of Monsieur Canada. Raymond Daniell.
New York Times Magazine. p 12+. Je. 17, '56. Eskimos meet the twentieth century. Tania Long.
New York Times Magazine. p7-9. Jl. 22, '56. Mighty task of taming a giant. Tania Long.
*New York Times Magazine. p 18+. My. 19, '57. Riding the Radar picket line. G. B. Jones.
New York Times Magazine. p39-41+. N. 10, '57. Canada evolves pro-Canadianism. Raymond Daniell.
*New York Times Magazine. p28+. O. 19, '58. Changing face of the Arctic. Walter Sullivan.
Newsweek. 46:80. Ag. 1, '55. Canada's major parties. Raymond Moley.
*Newsweek. 48:77-9. Ag. 6, '56. Canada's seaway empire.
Newsweek. 48:58. O. 29, '56. Tangled tongues.
Newsweek. 50:46. Ag. 19, '57. Troubled abundance.
*Political Quarterly. 29:114-23. Ap.-Je. '58. New course in Canadian politics. H. S. Ferns.
Public Opinion Quarterly. 21:252-64. Summer '57. Pattern of party voting in Canada. D. H. Wrong.
Publications of the Modern Language Association. 72:43-8. Ap. '57. Role of languages in the development of national consciousness: the Canadian experience. L. E. Couillard.
*Queen's Quarterly. 64, no3:326-37. Autumn '57. An offence unto charity: personal reflections on a national attitude. W. E. Swayze.
Queen's Quarterly. 65, no2:169-82. Summer '58. Causes of economic growth. J. K. Galbraith.
Reporter. 16:29-31. Ja. 24, '57. Canadian conventions: un homme qui. G. G. Harrop.
Reporter. 17:44-5. N. 14, '57. Introduction to a next-door neighbor. J. K. Galbraith.
Reporter. 18:22-5. Mr. 6, '58. How we stand with the Canadians. W. O'Hearn.

Reporter. 20:18-21. F. 19, '59. Canada's case of the American jitters. W. H. Hessler.

Rotarian. 87:34-5. N. 55. Gusher in Alberta.

Rotarian. 91:8-12. Ag. '57. Canada—proving its claim on a century. John Fisher.

Round Table. 46:145-8. Mr. '56. Canada and Asia; participation in the Colombo plan.

Saturday Review. 38:13. Jl. 30, '55. Review of H. M. Wade's *French Canadians, 1760-1945.* A. L. Burt.

Saturday Review. 39:26. N. 10, '56. For Canada and the world. Cecile Starr.

Saturday Review. 40:24. Mr. 16, '57. World next door. W. D. Patterson.

Saturday Review. 40:26-7. Je. 22, '57. Review of *Living Legend* by A. Phillips. P. Berton.

School and Society. 85:107-8. Mr. 30, '57. Canada's crisis in higher education.

*Senior Scholastic. 70:11-14. My. 10, '57. Canada; giant on our doorstep.

Senior Scholastic. 72:12-14. Ap. 25, '58. Canada, frontier on tomorrow.

Spectator. 198:373. Mr. 22, '57. British nihilists. Strix.

Time. 65:26+. F. 7, '55. Church said no.

Time. 71:31. Mr. 3, '58. Haven for immigrants.

Town Meeting (Bulletin of America's Town Meeting of the Air). 21, no8:1-12. '55. How far should Canada go in following U.S. foreign policy? M. J. Coldwell and others.

Twentieth Century. 161:556-60. Je. '57. In Montreal. N. Levine.

United States Department of State Bulletin. 37:718-21. N. 4, '57. Historic relationship of Canada and the United States. W. M. Brucker.

United States Department of State Bulletin. 38:294-301. F. 24, '58. Behind the headlines in Canadian-United States relations. L. T. Merchant.

United States Department of State Bulletin. 38:999-1004. Je. 16, '58. U.S. relations with Canada. L. T. Merchant.

United States Department of State Bulletin. 39:61-7. Jl. 14, '58. Problems facing the United States and the Western world; interview, June 23, 1958, of John Foster Dulles.

*U.S. News & World Report. 43:109-10. D. 20, '57. Where public funds pay for separate schools.

U.S. News & World Report. 44:72-4. Ja. 31, '58. Turn away from U.S.?

*U.S. News & World Report. 44:72-6. Ap. 18, '58. Frank talk about U.S. and Canada; interview with the Canadian Prime Minister, John Diefenbaker.

U.S. News & World Report. 45:29-31. Jl. 18, '58. New role for Canada.

University of Toronto Quarterly. 27:433-576. Jl. '58. Letters in Canada. Douglas Grant, ed.

Vital Speeches of the Day. 22:85-7. N. 15, '55. Don't take Canada for granted. G. E. Hall.

Vital Speeches of the Day. 22:344-7. Mr. 15, '56. Canadian adventure. N. R. Crump.

Vital Speeches of the Day. 22:373-5. Ap. 1, '56. Advantages of our mixed economy. J. M. Martin.

Vital Speeches of the Day. 23:335-8. Mr. 15, '57. Burdens we bear. S. D. Armour.

Vital Speeches of the Day. 23:693-4. S. 1, '57. Canada's American boom. R. A. Farquharson.

Vital Speeches of the Day. 25:280-3. F. 15, '59. How Canadians view the Seaway; address, January 27, 1959. S. D. Armour.

Western Political Quarterly. 10:733-5. S. '57. Roots of friendship and friction in Canadian-American relations. J. P. Vloyantes.

19845

THIS BOOK MAY BE KEPT

14 Days

and may be renewed if not called for by
someone else.
A fine of 2¢ per day is charged if the book
is kept after the last date stamped below.

DUE	DUE	DUE
APR 22 '75		
FEB 07 1985		
FEB 18 1995		
MAR 13 1995		